THE CALL
TO COMMUNICATE

MURDO EWEN MACDONALD

THE SAINT ANDREW PRESS : EDINBURGH

First published in 1975 by
THE SAINT ANDREW PRESS
121 George Street, Edinburgh EH2 4YN

© Murdo Ewen Macdonald 1975

ISBN 0 7152 0253 7

Printed and bound in Great Britain by
Morrison and Gibb Limited, London and Edinburgh

THE CALL TO COMMUNICATE

CONTENTS

Introduction

JESUS AND THE CHURCH

JESUS AND THE CHURCH

Thomas Altizer, the most celebrated exponent of the death-of-God theology, stoutly maintains that most of our religious headaches today can be traced back to the identification of Christianity with the Church. Theologians must ignore ecclesiastical structures and concentrate their attention on Christ as he is encountered in the totality of human experience. In other words Jesus did not intend to found a visible organised institution. The emergence and growth of the Church was an accident of history, fraught with disastrous consequences for mankind.

Malcolm Muggeridge, whose brilliance in journalism is only matched by his naïveté in theology, is an implacable enemy of the Institutional Church which he accuses of rendering unto Caesar the things that belong only to God. In a chapter in one of his books he addresses Jesus in the following words 'History is for the dead and you are alive. Similarly, all those Churches raised and maintained in your name, from the tiniest weirdest conventicle to the great cathedrals rising so sublimely into the sky—they are for the dead, and must themselves die, are indeed dying fast'. Muggeridge seems to take a wry delight in the immanent dissolution of the Institutional Church. Ignoring those passages in the New Testament that do not fit his own particular theory, he seems to equate Christianity with 'A Kingdom not of this world'.

At the other end of the theological spectrum stands Professor John Knox, the American New Testament scholar. He cannot conceive, of any form of the Christian faith existing apart from the Church. We may have some aware-ness of God either in our solitariness, or within some

3

peculiar social or cultural context, but our knowledge of God in Christ can only come to us within the historical community we call the Church. A denial of this historical community is tantamount to destroying the only ground we have for affirming the event of Christ. Knox stresses the indissoluble kinship between the Church and the fact of Jesus. He quotes Paul Tillich: 'Christianity was born, not with the birth of the man who is called "Jesus" but in the moment in which one of his followers was driven to say to Him "Thou art the Christ" '. Then Knox adds, 'Agreeing as I profoundly do with Tillich's emphasis upon the response of faith as belonging essentially to the objective event of Christ, I should yet say that a better moment to symbolise the birth of Christianity can be found in the Gospels. It is the moment when after Jesus' death a group of his disciples recognise in a divine Presence wonderfully new and strange the very one they have known and loved. "It is the Lord". In this moment of recognition the Resurrection became for the first time a historical fact, and the Church, which had been in process of becoming, since Jesus' first disciples were gathered about Him, came finally into actual being'.

Luke, the author of the Book of Acts, makes it clear that in the minds of the first Apostles, Christ and his Church are inextricably bound together. Perhaps both Tillich and Knox are going too far in emphasising a specific moment when the Christian Church was born. It might be nearer the truth to claim that it was God who created the Church, that its birth and continued existence were implicit in the event of Christ from the very beginning. To the early Christians, Jesus was the long-promised Messiah. By putting him to death the Jews had forfeited their claim to be the people of God. By the same token the followers of Jesus in accepting him as Messiah and Lord fulfilled the role of the remnant of which the prophet Isaiah had spoken. In other words the Christian Church was the new Israel.

If there are theologians today who assert that our first loyalty must be to Christ and not to the Church, Paul was incapable of imagining any such dichotomy. His claim to apostleship was based on what happened to him on the road to Damascus where he hoped to play havoc with the Church. Yet the words that stopped him in his tracks and haunted him all his days were 'Saul Saul why persecutest thou me?' As far as we know, Paul had no hand in the trial and death of Jesus, so the question put to him by the Risen Christ implies that Jesus and his Church are inseparable. And this is confirmed by the fact that dramatic as his vision of the Living Christ undoubtedly was, he did not go about as a lone wolf, promulgating his own individual version of Christianity. He travelled all the way to Jerusalem where he got the inner circle of the Church to confirm his claim to be an authentic apostle.

The choice of twelve disciples, symbolic of the twelve tribes of Israel, makes it clear that Jesus intended to create a new People of God, continuous with the old Israel. Liberated from the restrictive legalisms of the past, the purpose of the new community was to bring the world to a true knowledge of God. Significant is the fact that after the defection of Judas his place was filled by the appointment of Matthias. Thus the symbolic structure of the new Israel was preserved.

Jesus and the Church can be distinguished as birth and life can be distinguished but they cannot be separated. But now the question arises, what of the norm of the Church— this community which remembers Jesus and celebrates his presence through word and sacrament? Is there a model form which we can look on as the one and only authentic structure? Are all our ecclesiastical divisions distortions of the original blue-print to which Christians must conform if they are to take seriously the Church as the Body of Christ? The truth is that the organisation of the early Church is a highly complex affair. In no way does it smoothly correspond to our three major ecclesiastical systems—episcopalian, presbyterian, congregationalist—all claiming New Testament authority for their respective systems of government. It could be argued that in the Pastoral Epistles, the position of Timothy and Titus points in the direction of a monarchic episcopalian form of administration. Yet with equal vehemence it could be claimed that the Twelve Apostles seem to lean towards an oligarchic presbyterian system. But there is also evidence that the congregation played a distinctive role in the important decisions of the early Church. At the council of Jerusalem the congregation was by no means passive, and when Matthias was elected as one of the Twelve, one hundred and twenty members of the Church were present.

Gradually as time passed the three points of view tended to merge. This happened as the Church became increasingly exposed to the strife of heresies and the stress of persecution. It was perhaps inevitable that under pressure there was a swing in the direction of a strong centralised government. In other circumstances it would have been entirely possible for ecclesiastical structures to have developed in different directions altogether. What is more, other divergent forms would have been equally true to the Apostolic tradition.

In the very early stages of the Church's history there was no papacy, no patriarchate, no three-fold ministry. These, it could be maintained, were legitimate developments emerging from historical pressures and the demands of particular situations. But there is nothing essential or absolute about any of them. The authority and the continuity of the Church were safeguarded, not by a doctrine of linear apostolic succession, but by adherence to the Apostolic tradition concerning Jesus and his ministry, by the legacy of the Old Testament and the presence of the Holy Spirit. And today any Christian community which demonstrates these marks, whether it be Quaker, Pentecostal, or Salvationist, belongs every bit as much to the Body of Christ as those branches of the Church which have rigid hierarchical governments.

When we speak of 'unhappy divisions' there are certain unassailable facts which, in the midst of a very confusing situation, may help in giving us a clearer perspective. One source of distortion is our habit of using the word 'Church' to designate denominations or communions—Methodist, Baptist, Presbyterian and Episcopalian. Neither the New Testament nor the early church fathers are familiar with this term. They used the word 'church' to refer either to a local congregation, or in the universal sense to the whole body of those who professed Christ as Lord. The use of the word 'Church' as applied to a denomination, the early Christians would regard as anomalous, if not indeed unintelligible.

Again when we bemoan our 'unhappy divisions' the phrase is only superficially true. In the deepest sense all people who acknowledge the Lordship of Christ are already united. There is only one Church—the Body of Christ—and though its outward forms may differ to a maddening degree yet beneath it all Christians are aware of an indissoluble unity. In Glasgow University I regularly meet with a Roman Catholic layman's group who are concerned with the renewal of the Church. From the beginning I felt a greater sense of kinship with them than with many Kirk Sessions I have known. The truth is that we are living in a post-ecumenical era in which Protestant and Roman Catholic boundary lines are no longer meaningful. The younger theologians on the continent of Europe and in America have been aware of this for some time. For the rising generation many of the ecclesiastical issues of the ecumenical movement are of little consequence. The issues clamouring for some kind of answer are so gigantic that denominational proprieties pale into utter insignificance. Albert Van Den Heuval is surely right in arguing that unity will come not out of theological dialogue but out of the immersion of all branches of the Church in the secular world.

The Church is one, not only in space, but also in time. We sometimes talk of the Church of the New Testament as if it were an ancient monument shrouded in the mists of antiquity. But, so far as I am concerned, the Church reflected in the New Testament is not a strange historical curiosity; it is the Church I have always known. A few years ago I had the privilege of preaching in Fifth Avenue Presbyterian Church, New York, one Sunday and the very next Sunday in the church in which I was brought up in the Isle of Harris. No two congregations could be more dissimilar. One is situated at the heart of a vast financial metropolis, the other in a village, of which the big economists and the captains of industry had never heard. Yet in both settings, so glaringly different, I felt curiously at home. And the explanation, I feel sure, lies not in any possible likeness between the United States and the Outer Hebrides. It lies rather in the fact that in the twentieth century a congregation in New York and another in Gaelic-speaking Harris reflect something of the character of the New Testament Church. In reading the Book of Acts my primary experience is not that of learning something about the past, but of recognising something familiar to me in the present.

The Church is the Body of Christ, and its life is the continuation of the Ministry of Jesus. It follows from this that we get certain clues as to the nature of the Church's task today by studying the records of the public career of Jesus: his teaching and his acts. Here we are given a clear lead. The keynote is service: 'The Son of Man came not to be ministered unto but to minister, and to give His life as a ransom for many' (Mark 10: 45). 'But whosoever will be great among you, shall be your minister. And whosoever of you will be chiefest, shall be servant of all' (Mark 10: 43–44). 'But he that is greatest among you shall be your servant' (Matt. 23: 11).

When the Disciples are sent out on their own, their instructions are about the services they are to render. Jesus sent them out to proclaim the Kingdom of God, and to help those who were afflicted in body, mind and spirit. This is the Marching Orders of the Twelve (Mark 6: 7–11). This conception of the nature of the Church is not confined to the early ministry of Jesus. We have eloquent statements of the duty of the Church and in particular of its leaders in such passages as Paul's address to the elders at Miletus (Acts 20: 18–35) or his account of the ministry in 2 Cor. 3: 7, or the exhortation in 1 Peter 5: 1–5 or the charge of Peter in John 21: 15–17.

When the post-Resurrection Church began its work, two factors were present: (1) The Apostles were representing the Ministry of Christ who has taken the form of a servant and was obedient unto death, even the death of the Cross. These same Apostles were his companions in the ministry, and witnesses of his death and Resurrection. (2) The Holy Spirit, the Paraclete, promised by Christ is now given. But the thing to note is that Christ both logically and temporally is prior to both Apostles and Paraclete. It is as we realise the absolute priority of Christ in his Church that we see a ministry whose norm is the ministry of Jesus—servant of all. It is not possible to get any clear conception of the meaning of the Christian ministry unless we understand something of the nature of the Church—mystery though it is. And we would do worse than keep in mind the words of Professor T. W. Manson which he emphasises over and over again: 'The life of the Church is the continuation of the Messianic Ministry'. This is as true today as it was when Jesus came into Galilee preaching the Kingdom of God.

We cannot begin a study of the Christian ministry with a discussion of ministers and their roles in contemporary society. We must begin with the Church rather than with the individual whether he be clergyman or layman. It is to the 'One Body' that Christ has committed his ministry. This means that Christian ministry is not limited to a certain group nor is it the responsibility of an elite corps of members specially set aside. The Christian ministry is the gift of God to the whole Church as the Body of Christ. The current confusion regarding the ministry only reflects how far removed we are from the thought of the New Testament.

It is true of course that we turn to the Gospels in vain for a neat blue-print of the Christian ministry we can set down amid the ambiguities and complexities of the twentieth century. But though there is no specific programme laid down we are provided with many clues in the four gospels, in the Book of Acts and in the various Epistles. What emerges is an instrumental understanding of the ministry. The call to the ministry is not a bestowal of privilege or status but a summons to responsible work and witness. In their view of ordination both Luther and Calvin were true to this instrumental emphasis. No matter how many forms of ministry there may be they must all conform to the basic New Testament understanding of what the ministry of the Church is. Christian ministry is the response evoked when those who are gripped by the good news of the grace of God in Christ Jesus, feel compelled to communicate it to others.

BIOGRAPHICAL AND BIBLIOGRAPHICAL NOTES TO INTRODUCTION: JESUS AND THE CHURCH

Thomas J. Altizer
Professor of Theology at Drew University, USA. Author of *The Gospel of Christian Atheism*. A non-theistic kind of mystic.

John Knox
Emeritus Professor of New Testament Language and Literature, Union Theological Seminary, New York. Strongly influenced by Bultmann, though he disclaims discipleship. Author of *The Integrity of Preaching*, *The Death of Christ* and *The Church and the Reality of Christ*.

Paul Tillich
A German philosopher and theologian who emigrated to America after the First World War. Held Chairs of Theology in Union Theological Seminary, New York and in Harvard University. A profound theologian who was also a popular preacher. He showed a special interest in depth psychology, art and existentialist literature. Author of *Systematic Theology* (3 vols), *The Courage to Be*, *Theology of Culture* and *The Shaking of the Foundations*.

Part One

THE MINISTER AS TRAINEE

1. CALL TO THE MINISTRY

Ambiguity shrouds what we normally refer to as the call to the ministry. This vagueness no doubt reflects in some measure the crumbling of the cast iron certainties of former days, the revolt against ecclesiastical authoritarianism, and the fact that whether we like it or not we are living in an open pluralistic society where time-honoured sanctities carry less and less weight. It also reflects a conflict of theological traditions it is no longer possible to conceal. The exponents of the primacy of the secret call claim that it alone is adequate and dismiss ecclesiastical orders as so much presumption on the part of the establishment. At the other end of the spectrum the protagonists of the primacy of the Church call are inclined to reduce the importance of the decision enacted in solitariness. In addition to this there is the inevitable difficulty of relating Christian experience today to a theory of call, developed in the ages of revivalism and evangelism. This prevailing uncertainty may be regrettable but on the other hand the Holy Spirit may be leading us in the midst of our misgivings to a fuller understanding of what the call to the ministry really means. The issue is so important that we must try to dig down to the underlying theological presuppositions. So first of all let us examine the Biblical doctrine of election.

Perhaps the technical theological term 'election' has had its day. It might be better to speak simply of 'choosing', for the doctrine is only a more formal expression of what Jesus said to his disciples 'You have not chosen me but I have chosen you'. It expresses in the strongest possible manner the fact of the divine initiative in the process of salvation. We begin with the choosing of Abraham over all other men. Moreover, among the numerous descendants of Abraham

God chose Isaac over Ishmail and Jacob over Esau and of their progeny he established a nation. By normal human standards this nation was so small and insignificant that it was repeatedly conquered by the superior power blocs. Yet this tiny nation was the instrument of God's unfolding purpose in history. Hundreds of years later he narrowed the choice once more, to one man from this one nation, the man called Jesus. In this one individual, God chose a new people, made a new covenant and established a new Israel. This method of divine choosing is usually referred to as 'the scandal of particularity'.

This consciousness of being specially chosen by God, is a serious stumbling-block for many of our contemporaries. Arnold Toynbee, the eminent historian, lashes out at this creed with cutting invective. He speaks of the evil 'that is inherent in the belief that there is a "Chosen People" and that I and my fellow tribesmen are it'. He goes on to argue that western civilisation has been injected with large doses of this Judaic self consciousness as to our own unique importance. The curing of this unfortunate infirmity, he prophesies, will be the most crucial episode in the next chapter of the history of mankind.

We must admit that Toynbee and his fellow critics have put their finger on a real problem. We may well ask why God should have chosen to reveal his invincible purpose through one people dwelling in Palestine (an obscure backwater within the magnificent Roman Empire), a primitive provincial people who in comparison with the Greeks were so little versed in the higher arts of civilisation.

> How odd
> Of God
> To choose
> The Jews.

And to crown it all, God revealed the fullness of his grace and the essence of his being in a village carpenter. This indeed is 'the scandal of particularity'.

It is true of course that self-consciousness of this kind can breed an ugly arrogance, but on the other hand the great prophets of Israel did not leave the Jews a leg to stand on. Again and again they pointed out that it was not because of any special virtue or superiority they had that Israel was chosen. On numerous occasions, they proved themselves unworthy of election and had betrayed the trust God had reposed in them. He had chosen them not to be pampered favourites, nor to nourish their self esteem, or to inflate their natural pride, but to be his suffering servants in the world. The Second Isaiah who, perhaps more than any other prophet, dwells on God's choice of Israel, declares that the service to which Israel has been called is the enlightenment of other nations: 'I the Lord have taken you by the hand, and kept you, and given you as a covenant to the people, to be a light to the Gentiles, to open blinded eyes'. In other words God chooses an individual or a nation for a purpose which may spell self denial and costly sacrifice.

Next in importance is the need to clarify our thinking on what we mean by the word 'Ministry'. Our confusion is even more confounded by our inaccurate use of the words 'clergy' and 'laity'. We have forgotten that in the New Testament the words 'clergy' (*kleros* = share or portion) and 'laity' (*laos* = people) describe the same people. The clergy are those who share the inheritance, or those who are in Christ. Similarly the laity are the people of God or those who are in Christ. Bishop J. A. T. Robinson sums up the evidence: 'All that is said of the ministry in the New Testament is said not of individuals, nor of some apostolic college or "essential ministry", but of the whole body, whatever the differentiations or function within it'.

Professor Tillich argues that the Protestant principle, correctly understood, overcomes the gap between the sacred and secular spheres. It challenges every attempt on the part of ministers and theologians to set up a religious sphere separate from the ordinary secular world. He writes, 'There are in Protestantism only laymen; the minister is a layman with a special function within the congregation, and in addition to possessing certain personal requisites, he is qualified for the fulfilment of this function by a carefully regulated professional training. He is a non-layman solely by virtue of his training'.

John MacQuarrie, the Oxford theologian, though he does not express himself as sharply as Tillich on the issue, pleads nevertheless for a clearer recognition of what he calls the general ministry of the people of God. The clergy, he argues, belong to the universal ministry of the Church. They are laymen before they become clergymen. A layman is not a passive recipient of the Church's ministry. In Karl Rahner's words 'by the very nature of being a member of the mystical body of Christ, he is also an active co-operator in the fulfilment of her mission and mandate'.

The moment we hand over the responsibility to an elite group within the Church we find ourselves going down a dead-end street. One of our problems is the persistent misunderstanding of the classical Reformed doctrine of 'the priesthood of all believers'. In the past we have interpreted this radical doctrine almost exclusively in individualistic terms. In the New Testament we find the word 'priesthood' is not used with reference either to individuals or to a special group within the Church. It is used to designate the priesthood of Christ the King and Head of the Church, and again to designate the priestly function of the whole people of God, the Church which is his body. The Reformers stressed that all Christians had been called and constituted as a sacrificing priesthood, and therefore the gifts of the ministry are given and the task of the ministry is committed not to individuals but to the Church.

Though the fundamental ministry is the ministry of reconciliation and though there is no sharp cleavage between clergy and laity, the ordained clergy are looked up to as possessing a specific and indeed a fuller ministry. In addition to the general ministry which is the birthright of all Christians, the ordained minister is appointed the guardian of word and sacrament. Even in these traditions where he shares this to some extent with the laity, there are some acts which have been reserved exclusively to him. Among the great majority of Christians—Roman, Anglican, Lutheran, Calvinist— ministers are ordained only by those who have themselves been ordained to the ministry. In some Protestant groups, however, ministers are ordained by the congregation or general body of Christians. There are theologians, who argue that this latter method is not an ordination but a 'setting apart' in which the newly created ministry is regarded not as an 'order' but simply as a specialised function within the general ministry. Professor MacQuarrie categorically rejects this kind of ministry. It raises the question whether our attitude to ordination is in fact determined by our particular ecclesiastical allegiance.

In the western world there is an unspoken, perhaps un- recognised, assumption that somehow the clergy are in the Church in a truer sense than the laity. If, however, the ministry is given to the whole Church, then it cannot be delegated or dissipated in any way. It is the common responsibility of all. If this is so, why do we need a special ministry ordained in the manner Professor MacQuarrie argues. If ordination does not confer an 'indelible character' on the individual, then presumably it only sets a man apart for particular functions. All over the world, theological students, laymen and many young ministers are becoming increasingly dissatisfied with the traditional mystique surrounding ordination. They feel that above all doctrines this is the one that needs to be demythologised.

The view which regards baptism as the only ordination has gained wide popularity. Put bluntly it maintains that if all Christians are ordained in baptism a second ordination makes no sense. Professional ministers will be required, but even they should receive no further ordination. All we need is to authorise them to carry out certain functions for the good of the Church according to their special gifts.

Another view of ordination is one put forward by the

former Bishop of Woolwich in which he draws a distinction between baptism and ordination. Baptism would mark incorporation into the Body of Christ and would include communicant status. But ministry would be for all those who are prepared to take their Christian calling seriously in terms of mission and service. This would be marked by a rite equivalent to confirmation. All so 'ordained' would be equally ministers whether or not they later underwent training for specialist ministries.

Still further there is another view sponsored by Hans Ruede Weber in his book *The Militant Ministry*. Weber does not reject the position that baptism is the ordination of the laity. Neither does he reject the need for further ordination. He argues that, like an army, the Church needs pioneers, forging ahead, doing reconnaissance work, planning the next push. This corps, 'an apostolic mission to the church', would be made up of the ordained ministry. This insight of Weber may indeed prove to be fruitful but I cannot help feeling that the implementing of it would demand the most radical revolution in the ranks of the contemporary clergy. Not even their most ardent supporters would describe them as shock troops. Weber is of course aware of this and goes on to say that the 'special ordained' minister must be prepared to take up his position in the firing-line of militant mission.

I would be surprised if there were a neat, fully satisfying answer to the 'scandal of ordination'. When the early Church, under persecution, was pushing ahead, planning one mission after another, she was unduly preoccupied with the problem of ordination. In his *Church Order in the New Testament* Eduard Schweizer draws attention to the conflicting evidence which rules out all dogmatism on this issue. The picture of the ministry that can be constructed from the New Testament is a very complicated one and its interpretation is far from certain. Perhaps the only light we have at the moment is the urgency of mission coupled with the necessity of 'order'. The more seriously we take the Church's mission in the world the more flexible we are likely to become regarding structures and orders.

In his book *The Purpose of the Church and its Ministry* H. Richard Niebuhr distinguishes at least four elements in a minister's call: (1) The call to be a Christian, the acknowledgment of Christ as Lord; (2) The secret call, the inner compulsion which drives a person in the direction of the ministry; (3) The providential call. This includes the necessary talents for the job and the guidance of God which comes to us from the circumstances of everyday life; and (4) The ecclesiastical call, the summons extended by the Church or Christian community to engage in the work of the ministry.

Niebuhr argues that while the secret call, the decision forged in solitariness, is very important, the main emphasis of the call to the ministry is moving away from lonely encounter to the action of the community. In other words, the call is extended to social man, the member of the community, through the mediation of the community. As the conception of the ministry has changed from that of an elite group to that of the whole people of God, so the conception of the call has changed into that of the called and calling Church— the Church under the authority of Christ. It follows from this that the providential call assumes a new significance. The Church has to examine men and women to see which of them have been endowed by God with the spiritual and intellectual gifts demanded by the work of the ministry.

2. SELECTION FOR THE MINISTRY

Selection is not something discovered by a psychology-conscious culture. As an activity it has gone on ever since there have been organisations. In some form or other the ancient Romans had their own selection system when they chose centurions from the rank and file of their legions. So had the medieval guilds when a master craftsman had to decide on one apprentice from a number of possible candidates. Today we talk of job descriptions and job specification as if this was a brand-new discovery. The truth is that from the dawn of history employers had a fairly shrewd notion of the human qualities demanded by the work in question. Gideon's method of selecting the three hundred that eventually defeated a far larger army may have been crude by our sophisticated standards but it proved highly effective.

From the very beginning the Church employed its own methods of selection in its choice of leaders. The Book of Acts is not specific as to the particular qualities Barnabas detected in Paul when he strongly recommended him for the mission in Antioch, but that this was the right choice, the subsequent history of Christianity bears out. Until very recently each of the four Scottish theological centres had a panel which examined candidates for the ministry. The panel was made up of parish ministers, elders and one or two members of the particular theological faculty or college who more or less agreed on the qualities a good parish minister should possess. These panels may have been gloriously ignorant of modern selection procedures, but nevertheless they managed to produce ministers of outstanding merit and talent. Such panels or their equivalents selected men of the

calibre of Thomas Chalmers, Norman MacLeod, Alexander
Whyte and John Baillie. But while such a system produced
its giants it was also guilty of producing its dwarfs. It selected
men who, while intellectually respectable, were grossly unsuitable in terms of personality. They passed their necessary
examinations in Greek, Hebrew, Church History and
Theology but were incapable of entering into meaningful
human relationship with other people.

A radical re-examination of such an inadequate selection
procedure was bound to come. It was encouraged by
pressures impinging on the Church from various directions.
There was the new interest in the theology of the Church as
an institution in society. There were the insights of pastoral
psychology as to the mental health of ministers. These concerns were paralleled by a methodological interest in the
basis for vocational decision and the study of detectable
differences between effective and less effective ministers. In
addition there was the increasing incidence of 'drop outs'
shared by Jews, Catholics and Protestants alike. The recognition that piety and suitability are not synonymous, is
by no means a mid twentieth-century insight. In 1723, the
synod of Philadelphia of the Presbyterian Church recorded
of one candidate: 'Though we are satisfied as to his piety and
godly life, yet we think he wants necessary qualifications,
required in the Word of God for a gospel minister, and
therefore advise him to continue in the vocation wherein he
is called, and endeavour to be useful as a private Christian'.

It was no doubt in response to many converging pressures,
cultural, psychological, theological, that the Church of
Scotland decided to investigate new methods for the selection
of its ministers. The Education for the Ministry Committee,
traditionally responsible for the recruiting and training of its
ministers, appointed a sub-committee of which I had the
honour to be Convener. Our brief was to study various procedures, not exclusively ecclesiastic or for that matter
British, and report. Mr Tom Carruthers, Lecturer in
Psychology at Glasgow University, after a critical assessment

of selection literature brought back from America, advised us to communicate with the Civil Service Commission in London. In answer to my letter Mr Kenneth Murray, Chairman of the Commission, invited me to attend one of the selection schools as an observer. Mr Murray, himself a Scot educated at Aberdeen University, was impressed by the Church of Scotland's interest in a more effective selection procedure. He gave his promise that, provided the General Assembly authorised a modified form of the Civil Service method of selection, he would come in person to guide us through our first few schools. Appreciating that Mr Murray is one of our greatest living selection experts, the Assembly immediately gave its blessing. Thus the first selection school was launched in St Andrews in December 1966. Since that day every candidate for the ministry of the Church of Scotland is required to attend a school which lasts approximately two and a half days.

The term 'Group Selection' has been applied to this method. Perhaps a better description would be 'extended interview' with the procedure seen as a kind of prolonged interview stretching over two days, where the candidate is assessed in a variety of ways, including his effectiveness as a member of a group. The aim is to get as complete a picture as possible of the man within the framework of the different tests and interviews, to relate all the relevant evidence to his background, and in the process see more clearly his achievements in relation to his opportunities.

Candidates are assessed in groups of six with an assessing staff of three to each group. Two of the assessors represent the Church of Scotland; the third is a psychologist. In addition there is a staff officer and a secretary who between them see to the smooth running of the school. A Director acts as Chairman and moves from group to group during assessment to ensure parity of standards.

The school begins with the Director welcoming the assembled candidates, introducing himself and his fellow assessors, and explaining informally what the whole thing is about. The Director makes it plain that the tests are not of an inquisitorial nature. His aim is to dispel suspicion, and to establish confidence in the system before it has even started.

Over the next two days the tests applied vary enormously. The first is a Group Discussion. This is deliberately leaderless and unstructured. It is followed by a Committee Exercise Test where the candidate in turn has to fulfil two distinct roles: (a) that of Chairman presenting a problem; (b) that of a committee member contributing to a controlled discussion. The General Information Test is regarded as only significant when taken together with other corroborative evidence.

The importance of the Tactful Letter Test should not be exaggerated. If it does nothing else it indicates whether a candidate is capable of writing decent, simple English, so necessary in a profession which attaches so much importance to literacy. It also provides useful hints as to whether the prospective minister is sensitive to the feelings of other people. In the vocation we call the ministry, a certain level of intelligence is indispensable, but in the long run, it is not as important as a capacity for establishing a warm living contact with other people.

There are two Intelligence Tests which are never allowed to lead to final conclusions by themselves. If, however, they are used in conjunction with other tests they provide a measure of confirmation.

Most important of all are the Interviews with the three assessors, the joint interview with the two church selectors and the private one with the psychologist, each lasting fifty minutes or so. The Director also has a ten- or fifteen-minute interview with every candidate.

After the Director's farewell talk to the departing candidates, the separate Group Conferences begin. It is here that the bulk of the assessment is done and, with each candidate's score sheet before them, the selectors over a period of two hours arrive at a final mark, indicating acceptance or rejection. The chairman of each group sees to it that all points in the candidate's favour, whether in his past record or in his referees' reports, are fully weighed, and at the same time that hints of weakness are not glossed over.

Then comes the Joint Final Conference. Provided no unusual difficulties arise it lasts approximately one and a half hours. Candidates about whose acceptance there can be no doubt are dealt with quickly, taking no more than a minute or two. The bulk of the time is taken up with borderliners and clear rejects. Up to this point, the assessors have marked on performance alone, but now promise of potential is allowed as a relevant factor in the discussion.

Comprehensive and painstaking as the procedure is, the Joint Final Conference is not the end. Then comes the Report in Writing. Each assessor drafts reports on two of the candidates. He circulates them among his colleagues for criticism, so that the most accurate picture possible of the candidate may emerge in the end. These reports are valuable for a number of reasons. They sharpen the assessor's thoughts and save them from the vague discursiveness which mars so many references. They are also useful when dealing with a rejected candidate, offering a comparison if he appears again. And if the new procedure is to lay any claim to scientific validity, reports are necessary for any 'follow up' investigation.

A candidate rejected by our School is not irrevocably cast out forever. After a lapse of time he can come to another School. He will then appear before an entirely different set of assessors who have no access to his previous report till just before the decision is taken at the Joint Final Conference. It sometimes happens that a candidate matures over a period of two years and succeeds in making a very good impression on his second appearance. If in the interval, however, he shows no evidence of progress and his score sheet reads much the same as the previous one, he is rejected for a second time. All reports are lodged with the Secretary of the Education for the Ministry Committee and are kept in the strictest confidence.

I can imagine readers, however sympathetic and however impressed by the thoroughness of the system, wishing to raise a number of questions. 'Who selects the selectors?' This is a perennial difficulty. The ancient Romans asked: '*Quis custodiet ipsos custodes?*' There can be no completely satisfying answer but every effort is made to make the pool of selectors as representative of the Church of Scotland as is humanly possible. The pool consists of parish ministers (in the majority), lecturers, professors and principals of theological colleges, elders drawn from the different professions, and a number of women involved in the life of the Church. It would also be fair to say that the pool reflects a robust variety of theological emphasis. We have been alert from the start to the danger of selecting 'a stereotyped ministry'. If we are to speak to the whole nation, the church needs as wide a variety of ministries as we can muster.

It may be asked if psychologists are really necessary? My answer would be a most emphatic 'Yes'. Psychologists may not be superior in wisdom to ordinary mortals, but they are full-time professionals at the job of assessment. They have been trained to be consciously systematic in the difficult art of interviewing. In selection, the role of the psychologist is not to produce a selection process which is an inevitable part of the way any organisation works. His task is to make the selection decisions more often good ones. His job is to reduce the number of errors. The key word in this situation is prediction, because that is precisely what is being done in selection. The psychologist is hoping to predict how well or badly a particular person will perform. His task is to increase the proportion of correct predictions, by using a certain selection process, and by the introduction of techniques of prediction that are more valid than existing techniques. In the selection of members of a profession subject to considerable emotional strain, the presence of experts with knowledge of the structure and growth of human personality is, to say the least, useful.

Another question sometimes raised is that of the ethical

ambiguity of selection procedure. In the interests of the organisation, even if it calls itself a church, there is the constant temptation to regard people as packages, which can be measured, quantified and classified. The selector, be he parish minister or professional psychologist, must always remember that people are never packages. A person is subject as well as object. Precisely because a person is not a robot, there are so many factors within and without which render accuracy in predicting future performance impossible. A big powerful organisation, obsessed with productivity and the projecting of a pleasing image, is inclined to use the individual as a mere pawn to promote its own interests. It is no easy matter for a selector to serve the interests of an organisation that employs him and at the same time to recognise and respect the unique importance of the individual he assesses.

There is also the problem of the invasion of privacy. In the hands of experts the individual is induced to reveal more about himself than he would like and because his autonomy over his own life is infringed he often resents it. There are those who question whether any organisation including the Church has any right to probe too deeply into a person's inner life. What use is it likely to make of this private knowledge in the later career of its employee? While there is no completely satisfactory answer to this problem, the Selector must make sure that he never claims infallibility for any assessment system. He is more than a scientist, more than a dispassionate observer. He is primarily a human being, who while responsible to the organisation that employs him, must always respect the dignity of each individual—even those who are rejected.

One last question mark! Is there any guarantee that this elaborate, high-powered system is more effective than traditional methods? It must be admitted that no system is infallible, and that assessors, professional and amateur alike, are prone to make mistakes. But on the other hand, it can be claimed that the system, by virtue of its thoroughness and comprehensiveness, reduces the margin of error. At the end of two days, unsuitable candidates stand out more sharply, and there is a greater likelihood of the more suitable ones being chosen. In our church the system has been in existence for just over four years. No rigorous follow-up has therefore been possible. But over the years this procedure has won the confidence of governments, universities and big industrial combines. In the Civil Service and Unilever, where follow-up investigation is built into the scheme, it has been found that wastage is negligible and that the general standard of successful candidates is remarkably high.

There are those who claim that the call to the ministry is all that is necessary and that the human factor is not so important. This is a dangerous philosophy which, if acted on, would do great damage to the Church. A 'call' of course is of basic importance. But it is not enough. The Church of Scotland throughout her history has never proceeded on any such naïve assumption. In the past she has demanded a high standard of education from her ministers but erred perhaps in not more thoroughly examining the personalities as well as the intellects of prospective candidates. The 'Extended Interview' system of selection does stretch a man intellectually and at the same time it explores, as much as is possible, the whole personality. It is God who calls men to his service, but it is the Church, guided by the Holy Spirit, sanctified common sense and the know-how of accredited experts, that examines this call and in the end authenticates it.

3. EDUCATION FOR THE MINISTRY

As far back as 1575, Andrew Melville pitched the standard of education for the ministry on a very high level. A working knowledge of Latin, of mathematics, of physics, of ethics and moral philosophy was demanded of all candidates before entering on their theological course. The Church tried hard to adhere to the Melville vision of theological education, but in its wisdom it also made provision for aspiring candidates, who though they were not scholars, possessed other qualifications. Thus in the Presbytery of Skye permission was granted by the General Assembly to ordain one going to St Kilda who knew no Latin.

The momentum Melville gave to theological education in Scotland continued right into the twentieth century. No doubt there were ill-informed and uncultured ministers in the land throughout that period. Judging by the scathing remarks recorded by Boswell, Samuel Johnson must have met some of them and he was definitely not impressed. But the same stern critic admitted that the ministers he met in the Hebrides had good libraries and cultivated minds. They were such good company he says that he was truly sorry they were Presbyterians.

The nineteenth century also continued to produce ministers of outstanding culture. Alexander Whyte, born out of wedlock, had hardly any schooling. How he slaved to gain entrance into Aberdeen University beggars description. Yet by the time he was of middle age he was one of the best-read ministers in the English-speaking world. A cursory glance at his famous inter-leaf Bible points to a man of astonishing erudition. The minister under whom I was brought up, Dr Duncan MacLeod of Harris, was of a similar mould. His early schooling was meagre, but this country minister could teach Latin, Greek and Hebrew at university standard until he was eighty years old. I have heard Principal John Baillie say that when he passed through university the Church attracted a higher proportion of the ablest students than any of the other professions.

We can be justly proud of the high standards of theological education demanded by our fathers, but the question thrusts itself upon us, whether the minister of the future should be modelled on the Renaissance man, or on the cloistered Victorian scholar. Among theological students of all denominations there is a deep disquiet about the training they are at present receiving. They have a strong suspicion that theological education today is lamentably ineffective in equipping them for the task to which they believe themselves called.

Ever since Andrew Melville launched his educational revolution it has been assumed that the most important qualification a minister can possess is a trained mind. Provided a man is subjected to a rigorous intellectual discipline he is able to cope with every conceivable situation with an assured touch. This is probably what Arnold of Rugby meant by his famous dictum 'An educated man can do anything'. In prison camp in Germany during the last war I saw this truth dramatically demonstrated. Men steeped in a classically orientated education became skilled cooks, tailors, engineers and forgers. The trained mind invested them with a marvellous versatility. And if the disciplines of Hebrew, Greek, Theology and Hermeneutics between them produce a trained mind we should perhaps be not too hasty to despise them. Still, it is not at all self evident that the possession of a first class degree in theology equips a man for communicating the Christian faith in McLuhan's electronic culture. In the welter of confusion that exists regarding theological education, what if any are the signs of the time? Are we able to discern emerging trends that point us to the shape of things to come?

(1) I believe that all over the world and among many denominations there is a growing convergence of opinion that theological education should take place within a university setting. This does not mean that theological seminaries should be dismissed as pious anachronisms or that we should shrug off the weighty contributions they have made in the past. After all some of our most outstanding Scottish theologians, read and revered the world over, taught at our seminaries. Among them are such names as Robertson Smith, Lindsay, Denney, George Adam Smith and H. R. MacIntosh. And on a practicable level it is arguable that for ministerial candidates not capable of gaining university entrance, yet endowed with superb gifts, church seminaries are necessary.

While we may have to make exceptions here and there, it is fairly certain that the advantage of a theological education within a university setting far outweighs the disadvantages. Modern universities supported by the state have vast resources at their disposal. Compared with the church colleges they have as a rule better libraries and ampler opportunities for postgraduate study and research. In passing it is interesting to note that in America even the most affluent of the church colleges are beginning to feel the pinch.

Again there is the question of academic standards. The other major professions look to the universities for the training of their candidates. Doctors, dentists, lawyers, engineers and now accountants are taught within a university setting. That they have to send students outside for training in the more clinical and practical aspects does not in any way contradict this basic strategy. Similarly the Church of Scotland uses the university faculties of divinity for theological education while it leans on ministers, congregations and other groupings corresponding roughly to hospitals, law and engineering firms, to take care of the practical aspects.

One could also mention the highly diversified training demanded by the ministry of the future. A university is better able to provide this than any church college, however well endowed. In Glasgow University, for example, the Diploma in Pastoral Studies is made possible by the co-operation of no less than eight separate university faculties and departments. No seminary could be expected to have so many specialists on the teaching staff.

Not least of the benefits accruing is the independence theological education can have from church control. Robertson Smith, whom some regard as the most brilliant oriental language scholar Britain has produced, was deposed from his chair in the Free Church College in Aberdeen, because the Free Church General Assembly of that day regarded his views on the Bible as dangerous to faith. In other words they took away from him the life breath of the true scholar—that of free enquiry. Even when they are maintained by the state, universities must have autonomy and this acts as a bulwark against stupid interference and at the same time encourages openness to the truth wherever it may lead.

If it is to address itself meaningfully to our world, theology must not be done 'in a corner'. It must not be pursued in ecclesiastical ghettos far removed from the ferment of other passionate interests. What better place than a university for initiating discussion with atheistic Marxists and scientific Humanists. Theological teachers and students must not shelter in the catacombs of intellectual isolationism. They must emerge to engage in debate and dialogue with those who act on different presuppositions from their own. Such an encounter between theology on the one hand, and rival philosophers and ideologies on the other, lends strong support to the argument of teaching theology within a university setting.

(2) It is also important that theological education must take place within an ecumenical setting. There is a sense, of course, in which theological education in a university is already ecumenical. A faculty of theology in a university caters for all students who are academically acceptable,

irrespective of denomination. Such an arrangement offers a minimal ecumenical setting, but this must be supplemented by structures which the different churches must devise in the field of theological education. There is something comically absurd in the spectacle of a church college teaching theology ecumenically when all its students belong to a single denomination.

There are a number of signs that the denominational ice in theological education circles is beginning to melt. In the United States the American Association of Theological Schools have encouraged the coming into being of what they call 'seminary clusters'. In each cluster the seminaries would retain their separate institutional identities, but for educational purposes would function together, and would be jointly linked to a nearby university. Perhaps it is best to describe a number of ecumenical experiments of this kind taking place in the United States and in this country.

Union Theological Seminary New York is a good example of ecumenical co-operation. Over the years, the teaching staff has been drawn from a wide variety of communions, and students must represent every single denomination in Christendom. In Canada, Professor Charles Fielding of Toronto argues that the range of subjects handled in theological colleges demands a large and varied staff of specialists in order to avoid superficiality. He therefore proposes the closing of most of the existing theological centres in Canada, and the setting up of no more than five colleges with a minimum average of fifteen professors and about one hundred and fifty students in each. Such a scheme demands the intelligent pooling of interdenominational resources.

The existence of the Selly Oak Colleges may be as good a pointer as any to future developments. They are a federation of some ten institutions each with its own governing body, principal and staff. The impulse that brought them all into being is concern for the world-wide mission of the Church. The different colleges represent Quakers, Baptists, Methodists, The Church of Christ, Presbyterians and the Church

Missionary Society. In these colleges Roman Catholics, Orthodox and Lutherans have studied alongside Anglicans and Free Churchmen of all denominations. Every main Christian tradition and on an average about fifty countries are represented each year. These and other experiments all over the world are reminders that the death knell of denominational theology has been sounded. While its burial is taking place we find ourselves in the midst of ferment, wondering what the future holds.

(3) In theological education there must be no artificial divorce between theory and practice. There are theologians who argue that the theological course should concern itself with the theoretical and that practical training should be left to the various churches in institutions run by themselves. However attractive such an argument may sound from a logical and indeed from an administrative point of view there are a number of serious objections to it. Most professional schools within the universities—medicine, law, engineering—recognise the need for practical training and take some responsibility for it. Is there any valid reason why theological education should be different in this respect? But a more serious count against any contemplated divorce between theory and practice is the fact that theology is concerned not just with God, but with Man also—not an abstraction we call human nature but with man as he lives in the world amid its multifarious pressures and temptations. To divorce theory and practice is to dehumanise theology and consequently to embrace the docetic heresy in another guise.

This does not mean that we have succumbed to a narrowly pragmatic attitude to theological education. The 'kit-of-tools' mentality is prevalent among many members, laymen and even divinity students. They expect to leave university fully trained for every possible contingency—theological plumbers carrying with them all the tools needed for the most variegated job in the whole world. It just does not occur to them that situations change with such bewildering rapidity that a 'kit-of-tools' strategy can be positively disastrous.

Much more effective than the 'kit-of-tools' mentality is the functional approach. This demands professional integrity and thoroughness. It also asks for the application of canons of critical analysis to every problem and every challenge. In other words, theological education must be geared to the more basic functions of the ministry. The possession of an appropriate methodology is far more important than amassing a collection of sundry knacks and gimmicks. The latter are limited in their range of application and as a rule they soon become quaint useless anachronisms.

A common criticism levelled at the traditional theological education is the absence of a meaningful relationship between the various disciplines. For example, there is little or no relationship between subjects so closely connected as systematic theology and pastoral theology. In too many of our faculties and colleges the departmental mentality dominates. To put it another way, there is no integrating principle. I find it significant that writers as diverse in their approach as Richard Niebuhr, Helmut Thielicke, Hendrik Kraemar and Stephen Mackie are agreed that the integrating principle we are looking for is the mission of the Church in the world.

It would be wrong to write a chapter on theological education without saying something on a number of pressures it is no longer possible to ignore. One such pressure is continuing education. In this respect the medical, teaching and engineering professions with their periodic refresher courses have set us a good example. The thorough-going professional knows that his education is only beginning the day he leaves university. Private study and periodic exposures to a more formal kind of instruction are imperative if he hopes to keep abreast of what is happening in his own particular discipline. This idea is of recent origin in the Church and the response so far has been on the whole tepid and half-hearted.

In France, Germany and Scandinavia there are compulsory retraining schemes for ministers who have served five or ten years. In the United States many such courses are run by churches, colleges and specialised institutions (e.g. eighteen hours training in clinical psychology). In the United Church of Canada, before a congregation is allowed to call a minister, it must pledge to let him off one week every year to attend a refresher course. The financial responsibility should be undertaken by either the individual congregation or the denomination.

But why continuing education? Though it is important to know what is happening in theology, the aim is not to vie with the most recent graduates. More important by far is theological reflection on the ministry in the light of the experience garnered over the intervening years. This is the strategy employed by the Institute of Advanced Studies in America. It tries to help ministers to plot their positions and to re-assess themselves in the light of new knowledge and new happenings. Thus they can relate their theology more intelligently to the world in which they have to work.

Another inescapable pressure is theological education for the laity. The education of the clergy is very important, but the Church should not rest content with educating an elite corps while leaving the rank and file in comparative theological ignorance. The facts are somewhat disturbing: 99 per cent of Church members can be described as laity and only 1 per cent as clergy. The paradox is that while the 1 per cent disengaged from the world are theologically well educated, the 99 per cent involved in the world are theologically illiterate. They are unable to relate their belief in God intelligently to the crucial issues of contemporary society. It is therefore not at all surprising that more laymen than clergy support racial segregation. The explanation is not that ministers are by nature more sensitive to their fellow men, but that laymen lag behind in theological awareness.

But how is this possible? Isn't such a strategy too visionary, too utopian, ridiculously impractical? In a number of universities extra-mural courses are provided on various aspects of the Christian faith, but such schemes, though welcome, do not begin to touch the fringe of the problem which is gigantic in its proportions. What is needed first is a vision, for where there is no vision not only people but theological priorities perish. Whatever the merits or demerits of the Disruption of 1843, those who launched the movement had a powerful incentive. Within an incredibly short period of time they had established theological colleges in Edinburgh, Glasgow and Aberdeen and were soon producing scholars renowned the world over. If the Church is gripped by a vision of the importance of lay theological education, it should provide appropriate facilities, in co-operation with the universities or in its absence. The Church cannot prosecute its mission vigorously or intelligently until the laity become theologically articulate.

One last word on the desirability of joint theological education for clergy and laity. If the ministry belongs to the whole people of God, then it follows that theological education is a whole. The Northwood Consultation on Theological Education, arranged by the World Council of Churches, advocated shared courses between laity and clergy. It goes on to say that even when ministerial education is different in the sense that it is pitched on a higher level, there is no reason why it should take place in a separate institution from which lay persons are excluded.

This approach may demand a radical re-examination of existing structures of theological education. It involves the discrediting of two common assumptions which for centuries have been accepted without question. One such assumption is that there is only one kind of theological education. The other is that it can only be conducted at one level. By all means let us pitch our academic standards as high as possible for those who can profit from them but this does not mean that Christians cannot learn to think theologically in different ways and at different levels. The truth is that if we are to educate the whole people of God, we need a rich variety of theological courses. The mission of the Church calls for the maximum flexibility in training, and for a highly imaginative methodology.

BIOGRAPHICAL AND BIBLIOGRAPHICAL NOTES
TO PART ONE: THE MINISTER AS TRAINEE

1. CALL TO THE MINISTRY

Arnold J. Toynbee
Erudite English historian and prolific writer. His best-known work is *A Study of History* (6 vols).

John MacQuarrie
Formerly Professor of Systematic Theology, Union Theological Seminary, New York; now Lady Margaret Professor of Divinity at Oxford. He was one of the first to introduce Heidegger and Bultmann to English-speaking readers. A brilliant theological expositor, he would describe himself as a Christian Existentialist. Author of *Principles of Christian Theology, An Existentialist Theology* and *Studies in Christian Existentialism*.

2. SELECTION FOR THE MINISTRY

The Selection School reports its recommendations to a review body, The Sectional Committee on Recruitment and Selection, which is a sub-committee of The Education for the Ministry Committee. This review body has power to accept or reject the Selection School's recommendations and to propose suitable academic courses for the various candidates.

3. EDUCATION FOR THE MINISTRY

Andrew Melville
The man who in the sixteenth century made the church in Scotland presbyterian. He devised the theological curriculum which in the main has lasted to the present day.

John Baillie
Professor of Divinity in Edinburgh University (and brother of Professor D. M. Baillie, *q.v.* p. 68), his best-known work is *Our Knowledge of God*. His Gifford Lectures were published posthumously under the title *The Sense of the Presence of God*.

Marshall McLuhan
He has been described as the arch-apostle of electronic communication. Author of the controversial book *The Medium is the Message*.

George Adam Smith
The eminent Old Testament scholar who later became Principal of Aberdeen University. He combined scholarship with an outstanding gift for popular preaching. His 'Minor Prophets' were delivered as sermons to crowded congregations in Aberdeen.

Part Two

THE MINISTER AS THEOLOGIAN

4. THEOLOGY AND WORSHIP

Over the last two or three generations there has been a marked revolt against the practice of worship. Even those who unambiguously call themselves Christians have begun to question its value and relevance. On a Sunday morning they are found not in the family pew but on the ski slopes, or in the garden of their week-end cottage. The apostles of religionless Christianity look on worship not as a help but as a hindrance in preserving the faith and commending it to contemporary man. Scientific humanists regard worship as a survival of magic, an attempt even in a post-Copernican age to manipulate the powers of nature, to secure special benefits for the participants, by occult and semi-spooky means. Others still who would not describe themselves either as religionless Christians or secular humanists, castigate worship on the ground that it has become an acceptable substitute for action, an easy escape from the harsh brutal actualities of human existence.

There is a sense in which the practising Christian can sympathise with such criticisms. There is the kind of worship —not all of it outside the Christian Church—which is based on magical and mythological presuppositions. Its aim is to use God, or the powers that be, as objects to serve our own devouring ambitions. Again, worship can so easily become a separate self-contained department, divorced from the world and the issues that demand immediate attention. Then, the cult in which the Christian faith finds expression becomes something peripheral. Then, the building in which it is enacted becomes no more than an architectural ornament, or an ancient monument. Then, the community which en-shrines it has become a separate realm of the sacred to which men and women withdraw from the grim challenges of the hour. When this happens worship is no more than an escape mechanism and calls out for censure.

The Bible roundly condemns this caricature of worship. In the Old Testament the prophets thundered against it. In the New Testament Jesus and the first apostles had some scathing things to say about it. According to them, worship is no one compartment of life, no special area of the sacred, no sporadic activity taking place at the periphery of the world pressing interests, but something which lies at the very centre of our existence. Put in another way, in authentic worship the main emphasis is not on man searching and groping after the divine, but on the God who has created within the human heart the desire for union with himself. Worship is not a burdensome homage demanded of man by a proud omnipotent Deity. It is rather the free spontaneous response of man's spirit to the God who from the beginning has taken the initiative, and who in Jesus Christ became bone of our bone and flesh of our flesh.

But once we stress the primacy of the divine initiative in worship we must go on to admit that from our side the human contribution to worship is considerable. The character of this contribution varies from one particular tradition to another. In the more elaborate forms of worship a prominent part is played by music, architecture, colour and vestments. In the more simple and austere forms, as in the Outer Hebrides and the puritanical Protestant sects, these aids to worship are conspicuous by their absence. For the Christian there is no clear-cut choice between richness in worship on the one hand and stark simplicity on the other. Both can in fact be temptations to idolatry. Worship is idolatrous when it becomes an end in itself, when it is no longer a response to the divine but a paranoic projection of our own mundane ambitions and self-centred aspirations. If, however, we understand worship primarily as our response to the God who comes first to us, then we can welcome the fullest contribution man's creative skills can make to it.

If it is to ring a bell in the contemporary consciousness, worship must express itself in meaningful forms. All over the world, in the various ecclesiastical traditions, there has been a revival of liturgical interest which in time will no doubt assume a more definite shape. From the very beginning there has been a tension between fixed forms and spontaneity. There are those who argue that a set liturgy is the only bulwark we have against human subjectivity with its attendant aberrations and extravagances. Discontent with the bleakness of some forms of Protestant worship was bound to raise a number of questions. In the strong reaction against Roman sacerdotalism was it necessary to abandon colour, movement, and architectural beauty so completely? And what about free prayers? Psychologically speaking do they not create greater barriers in our approach to God than the set forms? From a psychological point of view, the threefold exercise involved in free prayer, listening to the minister, making his prayers our own, and then offering them to God, is by no means easy. On the other hand the familiarity of set liturgies can create its own special difficulties. For so many worshippers they are no more than an idle rote, lulling them into a soporific state of careless inattention. From the scrutiny of different traditions and the new readiness to experiment, people may come to see that free prayers and set forms are not mutually exclusive, but can be used together to enrich the whole meaning of worship.

From the first the Church was a worshipping community and the God it worshipped was one God, the God of Israel and also 'the God and Father of our Lord Jesus Christ'. But, as Professor John Knox argues, there are few, if any, universally shared forms of worship. For this reason it would be wrong to claim that one form of worship is right and that all others that deviate from it are wrong. There are churchmen who abhor Biblical fundamentalism, damning it as obscurantism of the vilest order but who fail to see that they themselves are liturgical fundamentalists trying to imprison the spirit of the living God within rigid and inflexible orders. In the renaissance of worship which we are now witnessing, we must stand guard against the dominion of the antiquarians, the self-appointed purists who suffer aesthetic torments if we dare alter one iota in the liturgies of Luther, Calvin and Knox.

While worship has assumed many forms and undergone vast changes since the first centuries, there are certain ingredients which are constitutive of its very meaning, the relinquishing of which would do irreparable damage to the whole. There must be a stationary element in the liturgy which is not at the mercy of any of our modern experiments, which, nourished by the tradition of the Church, links the twentieth century in which we live with the first century in which the Event we celebrate was enacted. Let us take these essential ingredients of Christian worship and give them a name.

One such ingredient is *praise*. This is not an after-thought, a mere addendum tagged on to the Christian faith, but an integral part of it. On the eve of the cross, Jesus in the company of his disciples sang a hymn. Writing to the Emperor, Pliny described the early Christians as a sect whose practice it was to meet every day and sing hymns to Christ as God. In his *Confessions* Augustine declares that in times of persecution the Church found singing an antidote to anxiety. The Reformers attached immense importance to praise. Indeed it could be argued that it is to them that we owe congregational singing as we know it. Luther was a hymn writer and though Calvin made no provision for hymns in his order of service, we stand indebted to him for the poise and simplicity of some of our best hymn tunes.

In an age which deifies the debunker, we must show discrimination in our use of hymns. Some of them are no more than outrageous imbecilities and they contradict not only what we teach in our theological colleges but the basic message of the New Testament as well. While we must be prepared to discard a number of them in the name of good taste and sound theology, we must on no account forget that faith in God must find expression in spontaneous praise. So it did the night Jesus entered the garden of Gethsemane. So it did when Nero unleashed his savage fury against the early Church. So it did when the Reformers marched against totalitarian might. And so it will always do so long as authentic faith remains upon the earth. Psalms and hymns are not sentimental luxuries—they are the folk songs of the Church militant. Christians sing them not because they want to impress their world, but because they cannot help it.

Another essential ingredient of worship is *prayer*. 'Without prayer', wrote Thomas Carlyle, 'there can be no religion, or only a dumb one'. This is true, but while prayer is the breath of faith and the Christian religion is not even conceivable without it, there are various forms of prayer which we must learn to recognise and differentiate.

There is a difference, for example, between public and private prayer and there is no point in equating the one with the other. There are brilliant conversationalists who are poor public speakers, and there are superb orators who are stammeringly inarticulate in a small group. There is an even greater contrast between private and public prayer. Both are addressed to God, but they differ in approach and method. Private prayer is intimate and the language used can be the simplest and most elementary. Public prayer is more designed and in the proper sense of the word more formal.

In the Church of Scotland where no set liturgy is imposed it is all the more necessary that our form of worship should be marked by seemly order and purposeful discipline. A congregation ought to know what is happening when the minister leads them in worship. The first prayer, as a rule, is one of invocation, and confession, ending up with an assurance of pardon. The second prayer, whether it comes before the sermon, or after it as in Calvin's liturgy, is one of thanksgiving and intercession. The ribs of a recognisable structure should stick out and a well-trained congregation should be intolerant of disorder or even the suspicion of slovenliness.

Another essential ingredient in public worship is *the*

reading of scripture. The Old Testament reminds us of the
'preparatio evangelica', the record of God's dealings with
Israel culminating in the coming of Christ. The New
Testament is the collection of documents produced by the
Church under the impact of the Event of Christ. From the
very earliest times the Gospels and Epistles have been used
as devotional material in private and corporate worship.
Within the life of the Church, they have had the effect of
emphasising the importance of its memory of Jesus and the
confirming of that memory to a worshipping community.

An ingredient of paramount importance in worship is
proclamation, *the preaching of the word*. As I am going to
examine preaching more fully in another chapter, my treatment of it here will be brief. According to Barth the word of
God meets us in a threefold form. There is the Living Word,
Jesus Christ, the embodiment of the Christian revelation.
Then there is the written word, the Bible which bears witness
to the Living Word. Finally there is the proclaimed word,
the voice of the Church witnessing to the Living Word, by
preaching and interpreting the written word. Preaching
properly understood is a rigorous enterprise, demanding an
intellect trained in biblical and theological disciplines, and
acquaintance with the culture of one's time. Thus the
minister is equipped to be an effective herald and interpreter
of the Word.

Finally there is the ingredient we call *the Lord's Supper*.
This rite has been at the centre of the Church's worship from
the very beginning. The Supper has many meanings, but one
of them is that of recalling and remembering Jesus. Before
the Gospels or the Epistles were written, Christians met and
remembered the death and the Resurrection of Christ in the
breaking of bread. John Calvin attached immense importance to the Lord's supper. In Geneva he did his best to get a
weekly celebration, basing the proposed practice on scripture,
but he was baulked by the lay magistrates. Calvin's intention
was to keep the word and sacraments in proper balance, but
as Protestantism developed, preaching came to have a pre-

eminent position. Of late there has been a reaction against what some theologians call the preaching lopsidedness of the Calvinistic tradition. While this correction may be justified in some respects, we must guard against a flight from the harsh actualities of a brutal world towards a sacramentalism which has become the special preserve of an esoteric clique.

In his *Religion in secular society*, the sociologist Bryan Wilson examines the phenomenon of liturgical revival and offers an explanation. According to him the minister of religion has been pushed out of the provinces which used to belong to him. Those were education, social welfare and pastoral care. Today the state, trained social workers and psychotherapists not only do the work which formerly was his but, what is even more humiliating, they do it much more efficiently. In the process of abdicating his traditional role, the clergyman has been forced to retreat to a liturgical citadel, from which nothing can dislodge him. Wilson is a professed agnostic to whom worship must seem an odd preoccupation, but his attack cannot be explained away entirely in terms of ideological bias.

We may not be prepared to go all the way with Bryan Wilson, but the charge he levels at liturgiologists deserves careful scrutiny. Every major denomination has its select coterie of artsy-craftsy devotees who keep reminding us, ad nauseum, of the treasures of music, architecture and devotional literature that have been lost over the course of the centuries. They seem far more interested in restoring the past to its pristine perfection, than in alleviating the malaise of the present. There is a kind of liturgical dilettantism which is an affront both to our intellect and spiritual sensibilities. Dean Inge was once asked if he was interested in liturgiology. Caustically he answered 'No, neither am I interested in stamp collecting'. The truth is that symbolism synthetically contrived and colourfully displayed is not within a thousand miles of touching the outward fringe of the human predicament.

What we have to rediscover is the real meaning of the

word 'Liturgy'. It is derived from two Greek words *laos* (=people) and *ergon* (=work) and was to begin with applicable to the world of politics and social action. In ancient Greece, instead of a citizen getting a summons to pay his rates and income tax he was more likely to be asked to do some public service like mending a highway, or helping to equip an army. This was his *lietourgia*. But nowadays when we speak of worship we think first of going to Church, and when we speak of service we think first of becoming involved in the world outside.

This is a false dichotomy. There is no authentic revival of worship, till what we do in Church is meaningfully related to what is happening in the world. Dietrich Bonhoeffer had nothing but contempt for the precious kind of worship which was solemnly enacted in a sacred niche, sealed off from the sufferings of mankind. He was condemning every expression of liturgical dilettantism when he said, 'Only he who cries out for the Jews dare sing Gregorian chants'. In worship, God meets us not at the circumference, but at the centre of our existence. But the centre where we encounter the divine is not a special region of the sacred. If our experience of God in worship is more than luxury, more than esoteric dilettantism, more than aesthetic titivation, it must reach out to embrace all the concerns of this life, including education, social action, and the taking of political decisions.

5. THEOLOGY AND PREACHING

It may be difficult to pinpoint the precise moment when preaching went into decline, but that we are witnessing its eclipse is beyond any doubt. In the last century and even up to the First World War in this one, the preacher of the gospel enjoyed enormous social prestige. In America a Phillips Brooks and Henry Ward Beecher, in England a Joseph Parker and Charles Haddon Spurgeon, in Scotland a Thomas Chalmers and an Alexander Whyte, were men of great distinction, honoured by universities, publicised by news-papers and listened to by influential sections of the com-munity. Today the situation is very different. The preacher has ceased to be a dominant force in the community and among the cartoonists he has become a figure of fun.

What accounts for this malaise, this deadly blight that has struck the pulpit in our time? It is of course true that we live in an age of affluence, and that television and other media of communication claim the attention of the public. Equally true is the fact that the preacher is a victim of sociological changes which have shifted the centre of existence away from the person to that of the structures of society at large. Nor can it be denied that the Church has lagged behind the spirit of the times and failed to keep abreast of intellectual progress. All this is true but these combined pressures, however damaging, cannot explain 'the sickness unto death' which defies our every attempt at diagnosis.

We may mount a massive programme of research, investigating the decay of preaching in our own generation. We may brief diagnosticians of the spirit of the times, depth pyschologists, sociologists, experts in communication, in a bid to probe down to the root of the trouble. And no doubt these experts will put their finger on many things that are wrong, but at the end of the day their pronouncements are no better than symptom therapy. The nature of the disease which has struck preaching lies much deeper. The traditional dogmas no longer command allegiance and doubts have deeper dimensions. The hunger in the human heart has been enlarged and will not be satisfied by a nostalgic reverence for the past, or by the kind of proclamation that disregards the traumas that have sunk deep into the twentieth-century consciousness.

The dilemma of modern preaching is that of credibility. The decay of religious faith is connected with a dislocation that has taken place at the centre of human consciousness. This dislocation has been brought about by the incredible increase of knowledge within a few generations. Human nature today is not any worse than it used to be. What has happened is that the new wine of burgeoning knowledge has burst the old bottles of time-honoured beliefs and sanctified orthodoxies. In some quarters of our secularised culture, God is an extinct concept, as extinct as Ptolemaic astronomy or Strabo's geography. The failure of religion seems to be its paralysing impotence in face of intellectual perplexities and moral ambiguities, clamouring for some sort of guidance. Behind the half-empty churches, the theological disarray, the common assumption that faith is no more than a distracting anachronism, looms the real crisis—that of credibility.

The task of the preacher indeed is a gigantic one. It is to do some justice to the ultimate realities, to speak meaningfully of the final mysteries and yet stand firmly in the twentieth century. Because so many pressures pound him and so many voices call him, his integrity stands in grave jeopardy. To retain it is a costly business. The negro novelist James Baldwin, who from bitter experience knows the price of integrity, once wrote, 'In my mind, the effort to become a great novelist simply involves attempting to tell as much of the truth as one can bear and then a little more —— The air of this time and place is so heavy with rhetoric, so thick with soothing lies that one must do great violence to language, one must somehow disrupt the comfortable beat in order to be heard. Obviously one must dismiss any hopes one may have ever had of winning a popularity contest.' The preacher of the Christian gospel cannot purchase integrity any less cheaply than the novelist.

It goes without saying that the most effective means of proclamation is the Christian life. It was in the life, death and resurrection of a person that God became fully manifest, and it is by the lives, sacrifices and triumphs of those who confess Christ as Lord that the attention of the world will be directed to the news the Church is commissioned to declare. Christian proclamation is not all oral. It is vital, involving the whole person. This is true, but when the proclamation has been painted, celebrated, sung and lived, there is still need for a thoughtful verbal explication of the good news of God in Christ. In authentic preaching there are certain notes which must on no account be muffled.

(1) *Preaching must be Kerygmatic*

It must point men and women away from subjective interpretations to an Event in which God has already spoken. Writing of the distinctive nature of the Christian message, Professor John Baillie puts it this way: 'It tells not of something to be accomplished but of something already accomplished. It is not a programme of "moral rearmament", it is news about reality. The New Testament does not say "Ye shall know the rules and by them ye shall be bound", but "Ye shall know the truth, and the truth shall make you free". Hence its fundamental proclamation (its *Kerygma* as it is in the Greek) is set not in the imperative, but in the indicative. . . . It is a tense that speaks of an action completed, of something that was done once, and once for all'.

The real meaning of the Kerygma, the nature of Christian proclamation, was brought home to me rather dramatically in prison camp in Germany during the last war. To begin with, all English speaking airmen were together in one compound. Then the Americans were moved to a new compound, adjacent to the British Commonwealth one and I was allowed to go with them as chaplain. Curiously enough we were allowed to talk to one another across an intervening double apron of barbed wire. The British had an underground radio and they were always in touch with the B.B.C. The Americans had none and so we were bereft of news. The British tried semaphore signalling, but it was easily intercepted. Then they tried shouting the news in French. This proved equally abortive. The next method was bribing one of the guards with tobacco and chocolate. It worked for three weeks but the poor wretch was discovered and sent to the Russian front. We were back where we started. It was at this point that some one put two and two together and solved the problem. There was one Hebridean in the British compound who spoke Gaelic and he could communicate in that language with me in the American compound. So at times of the day which were deliberately staggered, Corporal MacNeil gave me in Gaelic a digest of the B.B.C. news and I translated it for the Americans.

It was thus we heard the momentous news of the D-Day landing of the Allies on the beaches of Normandy. Early in the morning an American shook me awake, shouting in my ear 'The Scotsman wants to speak to you—it's terribly important'. I pulled on my clothes and ran over to the barbed wire. MacNeil just said two words in Gaelic 'Thainig iad'— 'They've come'. I woke the American camp, broadcast the news and the reaction was incredible. Men shouted for joy, hugged one another, leapt up into the air and rolled in the ground with wild abandon. The news they had just received convinced them that deliverance was on the way and that victory was in sight.

This is what the New Testament means by the *Kerygma*. The message the preacher is commissioned to declare is not a philosophy, not an ideology, not even a morality, but news of a mighty deliverance. In Christ, God has come right into the arena of our human predicament and the concentrated strength of the malevolent forces of evil are powerless to dislodge Him from history. The Event of Christ is not a theory, or a theological speculation but a fact as firmly rooted in history as the invasion of Normandy. Preaching which does not sound this kerygmatic note of 'happenedness' is inauthentic.

(2) *Preaching must be theological*

Any divorce between theology and preaching is a disaster of the first magnitude, yet there is a sense in which our divinity faculties have encouraged this split. Students, training for the ministry of any church, should be subjected to a compulsory course on the relation between the two disciplines. Heinrich Ott is surely right when he claims that theology is the conscience of the sermon. Theology is critical reflection on the Christian message and saves preaching from sentimentality and subjectivism. But with equal vehemence Ott argues that the sermon is also the conscience of theology. The proclaimed message, pointing to an Event, rooted in history, tethers theology to the solid earth. It saves the theologian from stratospheric speculation and relates him to the aspirations and needs of ordinary men.

It is significant that the big theologians—the real heavyweights—deplore any dichotomy between preaching and theology. We must never forget that Barth was a preacher before he was ever heard of as a theologian. It was out of the agony of preaching week by week to ordinary men and women in a Swiss congregation that his theology was born. If anything, Bultmann was even more emphatic. To him theology is a meaningless game apart from kerygmatic proclamation. He goes so far as to say that it is only in preaching that we enact Christ. Tillich, so philosophical and often so abstruse in his writing, was a brilliant and arresting preacher. It would be no exaggeration to claim that he and Reinold Niebuhr were popular preachers who packed university chapels and churches wherever they went.

In Scotland the divorce between theology and preaching

is all the more strange in view of our tradition. Thomas Chalmers, one of the most brilliant preachers of the last century, was also a Professor of Theology. MacLeod Campbell, claimed by discerning minds (including the late Professor Ian Henderson) to be our greatest Scottish theologian, was parish minister of Rhu and not a professional academic. To him, theology and preaching were as inseparable as oxygen and hydrogen in water. Professor H. R. MacIntosh, who occupied the Chair of Systematic Theology, was also the man who taught Homiletics to the students of New College, Edinburgh. And I can vividly recall how D. M. Baillie, in the middle of a closely argued lecture on some theological doctrine, would suddenly move over to the blackboard, and with a piece of chalk write the bones of a sermon, a model of simplicity and lucidity.

The Church needs the professional theologians, 'the back room boys', who stand back and can examine questions with the necessary degree of detachment. But she also needs preachers—field theologians—who are in daily touch with ordinary people. Theology as a subject is not widely read, therefore it is imperative that ministers should be so well trained in this discipline that they communicate it from the pulpit to those who of their own volition have come to hear. With theology, preaching shares the task of unfolding and interpreting the faith. But, with theological understanding, preaching brings other skills also, educational, psychological, homiletical and the like. Preaching, while inseparable from theology, has an ad hoc character all its own, in that it addresses itself to distinctive groups, where specific pastoral needs demand different approaches.

(3) *Preaching must be contemporaneous*
It is absolutely certain that the preaching of the first Christians was couched in the language of the common people. New Testament scholars have proved beyond any shadow of doubt that the language in which the early Apostles trafficked was the language which was spoken in the

highways and byways of the first-century world. The examination of papyri written in the years immediately preceding and following the beginning of the Christian era has shown that the Greek of the New Testament was the Greek spoken out in the world and not such as was normally used in works of literature. 'Christianity', writes Bishop Barry, 'was the first society which took the broken illiterate vernacular . . . of the Mediterranean seaports which no scholar would ever have dreamed of using as a literary medium, and made it the organ of a supreme literature'.

Paul the preacher may at times sound a trifle incomprehensible to modern ears, but the Apostle employed terms and concepts which were readily understood by his own contemporaries. What to us today are theological technicalities were to Paul's hearers truths put in a language which they themselves used every day. 'Freedom', 'deliverance', 'redemption' were words in common usage in the Graeco-Roman world where the number of slaves ran into millions. The concept of ransom was easily understood by the early Christians, many of whom had been bought and sold. Similarly with the idea of 'salvation' which for us has become tragically devalued. In Paul's time this was a word on everybody's lips. The soldier used it of a military deliverance, the sailor of rescue at sea, the doctor of bodily health. So when Paul preached the salvation which is in Christ Jesus his hearers understood him.

What we have to grasp is that the work of interpretation and contemporisation is a gruelling exercise. The preacher who is content with trite, hackneyed, conventional clichés is lazy and therefore unfaithful. The word we preach must put on flesh. It must enter into our own time and wear the dress of the present so that the people we address can understand and take sides. The supreme task of the twentieth-century preacher is to recapture the New Testament art of proclaiming the Gospel in the language of the common man.

The good preacher must be bilingual. He must understand the vocabulary of theology: technical words like Grace,

Justification, Eschatology. But he must also be able to translate this technical jargon into contemporaneous idiom, clothe it in the most appropriate imagery and communicate it as persuasively as he knows how. This need for up-to-date interpretation is vividly illustrated by Helmut Thielicke. He imagines a demonstration of the German Faith Movement with the appropriate anti-Christian agitation in Berlin during the Nazi regime. As the anti-Church tirade reached a climax a Christian in the audience could stand it no longer. He stood up and shouted 'Christ is the Messiah' but was completely ignored. But another Christian expressed himself in contemporaneous idiom. He got up and shouted 'Christ is the only Lord and Leader and without Him Hitler and all the apostles of this false faith will go to hell'. This man was mauled and torn to pieces because he was understood. Preaching becomes a living thing when the word is interpreted intelligently.

(4) *Preaching must be related to meaningful action*
Jesus fell foul of his contemporaries not because he proclaimed what the theologians call the Kerygma, but because he acted out the message he preached in a way that dispelled all ambiguity. He preached the Fatherhood of God and then went out to befriend publicans and sinners, the dregs of humanity and the scum of the earth. He preached the gospel of forgiveness, and in excruciating agony on a cross prayed over his executioners, 'Father forgive them for they know not what they do'. He preached freedom: 'The sabbath was made for man and not man for the sabbath', and proceeded to heal on the sabbath and with his disciples outraged religious opinion by walking through a field and plucking ears of corn.

This indissoluble unity between word and action is a precondition of credibility. Preaching in a vacuum, marked by absence of concern and costly involvement, deserves the contempt that our own contemporaries have so scathingly shown. Not everyone agreed with Albert Schweitzer's theology or methods of hygiene but wherever he spoke crowds thronged to hear him. Martin Luther King's appeal as a preacher was inseparable from his espousal of social justice and civil rights. And Bishop Trevor Huddleston is listened to in this country and elsewhere, because people know he is prepared at great cost to champion the underdog. The Christian faith will become credible when the message we declare is seen to be linked to courageous and compassionate action in the midst of the world.

6. THEOLOGY AND CULTURE

Up to the latter half of the eighteenth century, the word 'culture' meant 'the tending of natural growth' and by analogy the process of human training. Then gradually the word came to acquire new and important meanings. It came to mean 'the intellectual development of society as a whole' and later 'the general body of the arts'. By the end of the century, culture had come to mean a whole way of life, material, intellectual and spiritual. It is this later development which T. S. Eliot described so picturesquely: 'Culture must include all the characteristic activities and interests of a people, Derby Day, Henley Regatta, Cowes, the 12th of August, a Cup Final, the Dog Races, the dart board, in the pub Wensleydale cheese, boiled cabbages cut into sections, beetroot in vinegar, 19th century Gothic churches and the music of Elgar'.

In his studies on comparative religions, Mircea Eliade has made it clear that primitive man felt he lived in a sacred order which made sense of that part of existence which we call profane. His myths, rites and religious symbols were means which enabled him by repetition and enactment to transform the chaos of his profane experience into a meaningful and creative order. And the question we have to ask is whether the secular spirit marks the final dissolution of this old consciousness. Is secular man so come of age that he can arrogantly discard the myths which previous generations found not only meaningful, but necessary for the business of living in the humdrum, every day world?

Contemporary culture is radically this—worldly. Secular man does not see life as stretching out towards an eternal order, nor does he regard his fortunes as dependent on a

58

purpose, transcending time and history. He jealously affirms his own autonomy and freedom, his innate capacity to discover truth, and to create his own values. To him as to Feuerbach and Nietsche, religion is the sworn enemy of human freedom and autonomy. It devitalises man in that it makes him grovel in subservience, instead of taking control over his own destiny. This dichotomy between religion and man's autonomy is the recurring theme of philosophy, psychology, literature and even theology in our day. The suppression of freedom, still practised by some religious authorities, seems to lend support to this secular thesis.

The secular revolution has not come like a bolt out of the blue. Behind it stretches a long history, reaching back to the Renaissance and beyond. There are writers like Friedrich Gogarten and Harvey Cox who argue that the secular spirit is the historical offspring of the Biblical faith itself. Similarly we can argue that the new awareness we call the counter-culture did not spring up all of a sudden. Its coming to birth needed a period of preparation and gestation. It is the child of secularism which has staged a revolt against traditional sources of authority while preaching the gospel of freedom and autonomy.

However much we may deplore some of its most grotesque expressions, the counter-culture must be taken seriously by theology and that for a number of reasons. The Gospel has always been proclaimed within a particular cultural context. If it is to command a hearing, it must use thought-categories and an idiom of expression meaningful to its hearers. On the other hand there must be no total capitulation to the cultural mood of the age. Vigilance is needed so that neither side dominates. If theology ignores contemporary idiom and thought-forms, it will not be heard. If it allows the spirit of the age to dominate, it betrays its source and has little of value to offer. The former peril belongs to the European brand of neo-orthodoxy, the latter to certain versions of American radical theology.

The counter-culture is characterised by what has been

described as the emergence of a new consciousness. In his book *The Making of a Counter-Culture* Theodore Rozak attacked what he calls the myth of objective consciousness. The subjective side of human experience was despised while the objective approach came to be regarded as the *summum bonum*. Science did a great deal to foster the belief that in the pursuit of knowledge the intellect could remain absolutely detached. It had to remain neutral at all costs. If at any time, like Odysseus, it became suggestible to the siren's song of subjectivity it must lash itself to the mast of detached objectivity. But is this possible? It may be easier for a chemist, a physicist or a mathematician to adopt this attitude of detached objectivity, but such a stance is far more difficult for the historian, the psychologist and the social worker.

Collingwood had drawn our attention to the myth of pure objectivity, long before Rozak. The historian, no matter how hard he tries, can never be completely objective. A subjective element intrudes in the selection of the material under study and even more in the process of interpretation. Polanyi argues that objectivity does not exist, not even in the physical sciences. Despite these strictures, the cult of objectivity continues and its hold is still strong. Sociologists, psychologists and even sexologists like Kinsey, manage to convince the public that in all their investigations they are dispassionate observers, that in examining the most intimate of all human relationships, it is possible to remain clinically cool.

What Rozak and others challenge is the sovereignty of objective consciousness as the basis of culture. Any school of thought that belittles the poetic, the visionary, the emotional side of life, is guilty of the sin of diminishing the richness of human existence. The rebels are well aware of the strong influence the more traditional culture still exerts, but they are prepared to argue that we are witnessing the emergence of a new consciousness. The latter seeks to restore the vitalities that the traditional systems of education have so successfully repressed. These methods of education in the western world, may differ from one country to the other, but they all had one thing in common—the deification of the intellect and the denigration of feeling.

Rollo May points to the new emphasis which psychologists and philosophers are placing on feeling as the basis of human existence. Whatever the limitations of psychoanalysis, it has in no uncertain manner stressed the primacy of feeling. This is illustrated by Hartley Centril's paper 'Sentio Ergo Sum' which claims that this is a truer description of the mystery of human existence than Descartes' 'Cogito Ergo Sum'. Professor Alfred Whitehead, the eminent mathematician and philosopher, did not demote or disparage feeling as something which was merely subjective. He wrote 'It is never bare thought or bare existence that we are aware of. I find myself rather as essentially a unity of emotions, of enjoyment, of hopes, of fears, of regrets, valuations of alternatives, decisions —all of these are my subjective reactions to my environment as I am active in my nature'.

Many thinkers would agree with Whitehead that it is wrong to hold reason and emotion in stark antithesis. On the contrary, scientific discovery and artistic inspiration seem to form a continuum and the boundary line between the two activities is always a fluid one. There are two levels of awareness. The one operates in broad daylight, the other much deeper down, among what Jung calls the region of the archaic and archetypal images. Cerebral analytical thinking involves a single frame of reference. Faith, which is never divorced from the intellect, involves more than one.

The new consciousness is hospitable to the place of feeling in religious awareness. It recognises feeling as a mode of awareness, underlying and reaching beyond all conceptual thinking and all attempts at articulation. If there are thoughts too deep for words, there are feelings too deep for formal thinking. As a rule theologians are frightened of facing up to the emotional side of religion. The way they normally articulate the Christian faith does not evoke an authentic emotional response, hence the rise of Pentecostalism and the Jesus Movement. Unless the Christian revelation is related to the depth of our human experience, it will not be revelation at all, but a disembodied bloodless abstraction.

An integral part of this new consciousness is the youth-culture which has emerged in America, in Britain and indeed in practically all modern pluralistic societies. The particular aspects of this culture may vary from place to place and from time to time, but certain broad features are similar. The most outstanding features are its distinctive aesthetic styles. Whatever the youth fashion may be, in dress, in music, in mannerisms and style, it stands in sharp contrast to the fashion of the more adult members of the same society. This indeed may be the real function of youth culture, the asserting of its independence against adult dominance and authority. Youth culture has helped to reduce social barriers and at the same time to increase the barriers between the young and the old within the same social class. This is what some writers mean when they claim—perhaps somewhat extravagantly—that the most important social barriers are no longer those of class, but those of age.

The counter-culture is distinguished by its style of dress. The drab, rather unkempt, clothes are supposed to symbolise profound democratic values. They represent no distinctions of wealth, status or elitism. In the older cultures a banker, a lawyer, a business executive, or any member of the traditional professional classes could be recognised by his well cut, rather expensive clothes. Tailored distinctions pointed to social differentiations, to cultural superiority, and to jealously guarded disadvantages. The new style of dress has declared war on these age-old assumptions. It is hostile to any hierarchical social structure, symbolised and indeed sancti-fied by the kind of clothes people wear.

The counter-culture is also distinguished by an entirely new attitude to drugs. Eminent Victorians like Coleridge, Rosetti and Dickens were addicted to laudanum and morphine, but on the whole the society of that time was tolerant to its drug-taking literary luminaries. But no similar tolerance was shown to the John Lennons and Mick Jaggers of post-war Britain. The explanation seems to be that drug-taking Victorian writers were social conformists whereas the apostles of the counter-culture represent an ethos of dis-affiliation that threatened the stability of society. Aldous Huxley also experimented with mescaline in order to delve deeper into the mystery of human consciousness. Timothy Leary, more rash than Huxley, promised the world 'a psychedelic revolution' and claimed that the universal use cf L.S.D. would change society in the most radical manner imaginable. To many who are by no means opposed to all expressions of the counter-culture this is indeed a shuddering prospect. If the habitual users of hard drugs represent the new humanity, may God have mercy on us all.

Of all the media used by the counter-culture, music is perhaps the most expressive. The older generation, bound by their own tradition, are scathingly critical of what they dismiss as a cacophony of incoherent sounds. But there are musical connoisseurs who speak highly of its quality and technical sophistication. Its appeal is enormous and it has the power to communicate across every barrier—race, culture, geography. In a restaurant in Britain, America, Russia or Scandinavia, let some one put a coin in a juke-box and young people begin to drum fingers and tap feet, oblivious of the country where the particular tune may have originated. Furthermore this kind of music is not divorced from social concern. It is sometimes more sensitive to injustice, alienation and the terror of meaninglessness than many of our sociologists, journalists and best selling novelists. The secret of its universal appeal may lie in the fact that it speaks to our condition.

There is one other expression of the counter-culture which must on no account be ignored and that is the revolt against the University as an institution in our society. Not so long ago intellectuals were inclined to regard the Church as the bastion of reaction and a purveyor of implausible myths, while they looked upon the University as the epitome of all that was rational and enlightened. Whatever we mean by the counter-culture, it has stood this kind of thinking on its head. To a former generation, the Church was the institution under siege. To the new generation it is the University which is under moral and intellectual fire. What the Church was to eighteenth-century radicals, to Voltaire of France, and Hume of Scotland, so the University has become to the rebels of our day, the new Left, the social agitators and the disenchanted students of every continent.

The rebels claim that the University, while it prides itself on its capacity to demythologise, itself sponsors a number of squalid myths which cannot stand up to intelligent scrutiny. Claiming to be the champion of secularity in all its myriad forms, the University had contracted out of costly involve-ment in the secular world. Its much-vaunted neutrality is just escapism and dishonest rationalisation. Its disengage-ment from the world is not in the interests of pure research, but in that of securing for itself a privileged niche in our affluent society. The University may study society in an abstract entity but in the revolutions that convulse our age, it is found sitting on the grandstand, not doing battle in the arena.

The other charge levelled against the University is its alleged hypocrisy. While preaching a gospel of other worldly transcendence, the medieval Church committed every crime in the calendar to further its own selfish interests in this world. According to the apostles of the counter-culture, the University, behind its mask of rationality and objectivity, is guilty of a similar betrayal. This, they claim, has happened in Russia, where universities supposedly committed to free enquiry have kow-towed to obscurantist ideologies. It happened in Nazi Germany and according to the rampaging students of Berkeley, California, and Columbia, New York, it has happened in America. Surely one of the most intriguing ironies of modern history is that at the moment, the icono-clasts the world over are more hostile to the University than they are to the Church.

Critique of Counter-Culture

Christian theology ought not to be unduly surprised by talk of radical change. After all, the faith it expounds promised 'If any man be in Christ he is a new creation'. From the very beginning the Christian Gospel has been preoccupied with *metanoia*, repentance, new turnings and revolutions in people's lives. While certain expressions of the new cultural promise are deplored, there are other features of it which must elicit response from thoughtful Christians. In the many books written on this subject there has emerged a consensus of opinion that somewhere among the premature and partial visions we are witnessing the emergence of a new consciousness.

It could be argued that one weakness of the counter-culture is its contempt for the past. The romantic dream of simply starting anew, and by that means escaping all the distortions of the past, is illusory. The most drastic changes in society inevitably preserve many elements both cultural and structural from the old order. The first Christians did not regard the Church as a creation *ex nihilo*. It was the New Israel, embodying and observing all that was best in the witness of the prophets and martyrs. The same was true of the Reformation. Though they introduced radical innovations, Luther and Calvin did not discard the structures of the old order. Like the early Church, the new revolution was a process of continuity and discontinuity.

By the same token the counter-culture cannot possibly shake off the weight of the past. Rozak defined it as 'a culture so radically disaffiliated from the mainstream assumptions of our society that it scarcely looks to many as a culture at all, but takes on the alarming appearance of a barbaric intrusion'. This indeed may prove to be the Achilles' heel of the counter-culture. The prophets of a new consciousness, advocates of a complete break with past history, talking of an evolutionary leap, a new step in the psycho-genetic history of man, may have forgotten that the Nazis before them used similar grandiloquent terms. The history of the past may not be all that glorious, but only fools and madmen will try to forget it. There can be no cultural advance which forgets that history proceeds by a dynamic process of continuity and discontinuity.

It could be further argued that another weakness of the counter-culture is its contempt for the intellect. That is one reason, among many more valid ones, why the University is under attack. The University is castigated as the enemy of feeling, of intuition and all that we mean by the subjective. This may be a valid criticism but those who make it should go on to ask if any culture can survive if it is not subjected to critical enquiry. However disenchanted we may be with our universities, Michael Novak's observation must be taken seriously: 'unless the university has somewhere among its various novelties and institutes for relevance, a cadre of men, committed to the demands of critical intelligence, little in the university can be of enduring relevance'.

The prophets of the counter-culture may despise critical enquiry, but how can any society subsist without it? Critical enquiry is not something conducted in an ivory tower. On the contrary it is something which examines every form of human activity including universities and it is prepared to ask awkward questions without deference to contemporary relevance. It will examine the Church and its sanctified pretensions, democracy with all its manifold myths, culture, counter or otherwise, which remains blind to its own defects. Critical enquiry is no respecter of persons. It cannot be manipulated by pressure groups. It recognises no sanctified precincts, no sacred niches, no holy of holies. Over the extravagancies of the counter-culture it stands like a flaming angel, and it shows no mercy on sloppy sentimentalism.

Finally, we could argue that the counter-culture is woefully volatile. In a devastating attack, Michael Novak lists a number of signs which point to the transitoriness and perhaps the utter dissolution of the counter-culture. One such is the attributing of satanic motives to all who refuse to become camp followers of the cultural avant-garde, and the paranoic abuse heaped on those who oppose the movement. Another is the sporadic outbursts of violence, indicating a basic insecurity and an impoverishment of intellect and imagination. Another still is the parasitic nature of the counter-culture. It feeds on the vile body it despises and presumably seeks to destroy. Finally there is the fissiparous sectarianism which has marked it all along. The movement is divided, confused, depressed and the forces of death are everywhere. Novak may be over-confident in predicting its complete and utter dissolution, but so far it has offered no convincing proof that it can disestablish the past and usher in a new heaven and a new earth.

The Christian Church has always witnessed within a particular cultural context, so in order to proclaim intelligently it must be sensitive to the world in which it exists. But under the suffocating pressure of relevance, the Church may become too worldly in the bad sense of that word. The Church has failed to disturb our culture by a prophetic word of judgment and of healing, because it has become a mere mirror of that culture, hence the danger of slogans like 'worldly Christianity'. Christians must witness within the structures of the secular world, but they must also have an awareness of the holy and the transcendent. Jesus has been truly described as 'the man for others' but the same Jesus made time for corporate worship and private prayer, so that he might live more truly for others. Bonhoeffer rightly warned us that we ought not to be more religious than God but someone should also warn us that we ought not to be more worldly than Jesus.

BIOGRAPHICAL AND BIBLIOGRAPHICAL NOTES
TO PART TWO: THE MINISTER AS THEOLOGIAN

4. THEOLOGY AND WORSHIP

Karl Barth

Generally regarded as the foremost theologian of the twentieth
century. His massive work *Dogmatics* stresses the sinfulness of man,
the holiness and transcendence of God, the importance of revelation and the salvation which resides in Christ alone. Though a
courageous opponent of Nazism, he refused to regard the Communist East as more sinful than the so-called Christian West.

Dietrich Bonhoeffer

The German theologian and martyr who was, to begin with, a
disciple of Barth. Described as the chief apostle of secular
Christianity, his best-known work is his posthumous *Letters and
Papers from Prison*.

5. THEOLOGY AND PREACHING

Heinrich Ott

A German theologian who succeeded Barth at Basle. His book
Theology and Preaching is an apologia for the indissoluble relationship between the two disciplines.

D. M. Baillie

Professor of Theology in St Andrews University and brother of
John Baillie (*q.v.* p. 37). His best-known work is *God was in
Christ*. There were three posthumous books: *Sacramental Theology*
and two volumes of sermons *To Whom Shall We Go?* and *Out of
Nazareth*.

Helmut Thielicke

The German theologian who is also an outstanding popular
preacher, a fact which shows that the two pursuits are in no way
incompatible. Author of *The Ethics of Sex*, *The Waiting Father* and
The Trouble with the Church.

6. THEOLOGY AND CULTURE

R. G. Collingwood
Perhaps his best-known work is *The Idea of History*. Collingwood debunked the claim that the study of history can be a dispassionately objective discipline. The element of subjective interpretation is ever present.

Michael Polyani
In his books *Personal Knowledge* and *Tacit Dimensions* he claims what we do is based on a certain kind of 'knowing'. This knowledge is not amenable to precise logical or scientific analysis.

Rollo May
An American existentialist psychoanalyst. While admitting his debt to Freud, he differs from him in drawing a clear distinction between sexuality and love. His best-known work is *Love and Will*.

Alfred Whitehead
A friend and collaborator of Bertrand Russell, he became Professor of Philosophy in Harvard University. His best-known works are *Process and Reality* and *The Adventure of Ideas*. The exponents of Process Theology like Norman Pittinger and Schubert Ogden acknowledge their indebtedness to him.

Part Three

THE MINISTER AS TEACHER

7. CINDERELLA STATUS OF THE TEACHING MINISTRY

Among the various ministries recognised and exercised by the Church the teaching ministry is the cinderella of them all. Such a phenomenon is all the more difficult to understand when we think of the long history of teaching that lies behind the Christian faith. Its roots can be traced back to the Old Testament which placed a strong emphasis on ethical and religious instruction in home and community. The Rabbi, as a recognised professional teacher, was a revered figure in the land. Within the Jewish culture he commanded more respect than a university professor does in Scotland today. This tradition was carried over into the New Testament. It is surely significant that his own contemporaries referred to Jesus as a Rabbi. They were paying him the highest compliment known to them when they called him a Teacher come from God.

Traditionally, in theory anyhow, the Protestant Church attached great importance to catechetical instruction. In the Hebrides, children were drilled in the shorter catechism in both English and Gaelic, at home and at school. This was done with such thoroughness that even now I can repeat screeds on justification, sanctification and election without taxing my memory. The fact remains, however, that with the exception of isolated pockets in our culture, the Protestant laity are appallingly illiterate. I can recall an American Rhodes Scholar, in the middle of a public debate in prison camp, quoting from what he authoritatively referred to as the Book of Jacob. When I pointed out that such a book did not exist, he was genuinely surprised. What I found even more disconcerting was that the bulk of the audience, nearly all college graduates, were equally ignorant.

We talk a great deal about Evangelism. Books in plenty are written on the subject on both sides of the Atlantic. The assumption underlying many of them is that 'insiders'—those who confess Christ as Lord are in a position to convey the truth about Christianity to 'outsiders'. The truth is that the vast majority of Church members have but the flimsiest notions of what the basic tenets of the Christian faith are. At the same time governments, all over the world, are pushing ahead with ambitious educational programmes. They are building new schools, new libraries, new colleges and universities. Opportunities for higher education are open as never before in our history. Knowledge is multiplying at an astonishing rate and the intelligent are actively encouraged by state-aided grants. The paradoxical situation is like an inverse ratio sum in arithmetic—the more secular knowledge expands the less religious knowledge grows. If the ever-widening chasm continues, the prospects are exceedingly bleak.

Indeed we could argue that many of the semi-religious ideologies, invoked to support and sanctify monstrous injustices in our day and age, are the result of inadequate Christian teaching. In South Africa educated people use the Bible to bolster apartheid. In Belfast at a ministers' conference I incurred considerable displeasure when I said the Orange Lodge was not a Christian order. In this country there are any number of Christians, labouring under illusions equally absurd. It is difficult to blame them. From infancy they have not been brought face to face with the disturbing implications of the Christian gospel.

The subordination of the teaching ministry has become part of our culture. It has come to be unconsciously accepted by members, office bearers, ministers and the courts of the Church. Let a minister refuse to preach and he will soon run foul of the appropriate authorities. Let him refuse to celebrate the sacraments and in no time he will be arraigned before some ecclesiastical court. Let him reach a certain level of administrative incompetence, which includes the collecting of money, and he is asking for trouble. Let him decline to visit the sick, tend those in trouble, officiate at funerals, exercise a modicum of pastoral care, and he is anathematised throughout the entire community. But teaching is in a different category. Not only can a minister survive its total neglect, but providing of course he performs his other duties with a reasonable degree of competence, he can attain to the very highest honours the Church can confer on him. As things are at the moment the teaching ministry is optional. A minister may choose to teach or not to teach.

There are visible signs and symbols of the subordinate status of the teaching ministries in our Churches. Consider the disproportionate amount of money the Church is prepared to spend on beautifying the sanctuary as against the pitiful sum she doles out on equipping classrooms, acquiring visual aids and modern media of communication. Office-bearers who will haggle over a few pounds to buy the most rudimentary equipment for the young, will cheerfully raise thousands for an organ, a font or the construction of a more elegant chancel. Too often the aesthetic impressiveness of the sanctuary stands in sharp contrast to the squalid drabness of the classroom.

There is also a startling antithesis between the theological education of the minister and that of the average Sunday School teacher. The minister of word and sacrament had to be an educated man. Only after he has been subjected to a fairly rigorous intellectual training is he allowed to go forward to ordination. But in Sunday Schools and Bible Classes, anyone can instruct the young and the impressionable however untutored and unenlightened. At our theological colleges ministers are taught to look at the Bible in the light of the latest historic scientific research. Our children on the other hand are left to the mercy of a naïve obscurantist fundamentalism and we seem powerless to break through the vicious circle. The ministry of word and sacrament merits ordination. The bringing up of the young in the nurture and admonition of the Lord apparently does not.

How do we explain the subordination of the teaching ministry of the Church? Why is it that for centuries on end discerning people have come to terms with its cinderella status without a murmur of protest? Why do we loudly deplore the prevailing ignorance regarding all things religious and fail to take practical steps to correct this strange anomaly? How do we account for this built-in complacency?

One fairly obvious reason is that from the very beginning the ministry of word and sacrament has been regarded as distinctively and peculiarly charismatic. Behind this attitude there lurks the deeply entrenched dichotomy between Grace and Truth. The former is supposed to be charismatic, the latter not. In his searching book *Church Order in the New Testament* Eduard Schweizer argues that Paul refused to draw any such distinction. According to the apostle the only valid criterion of an authentic ministry was whether it edified people and helped them to grow in the faith. In this age of burgeoning knowledge it is sheer lunacy on the part of the Church to soft-peddle Truth, or accord it a subordinate status. What is more we must be prepared to savagely scrutinise any theology that holds up Truth in antithesis to Grace.

Another reason for its subordination is the offence inherent in the teaching ministry. It is possible to preach vague ponderous generalities about the love and the justice of God which leave hearers slumbering in their habitual complacency. But when the practical implications of the message are spelt out with unambiguous clarity, people are compelled to take sides. So it was with the Old Testament prophets. They preached righteousness and then proceeded to spell out what that meant in terms of power politics for Israel. Jeremiah would never have got into trouble if he had not been so disconcertingly down to earth in his teaching. The same is true of Jesus himself, who was a teacher as well as a preacher. It was when he spelt out and made explicit his views on the sabbath, his contempt of ceremonial purification and neurotic moral scrupulosity, his attitude to dishonest trafficking in the temple that he incurred the implacable hostility of the establishment.

This is not a phenomenon peculiar to Biblical times. It has happened again and again in the course of history. John Huss, Martin Luther, George Wishart and many more who faithfully expounded the truth as they saw it, aroused massive opposition. Professor Robertson Smith would have lived and enjoyed an uneventful, tranquil academic career had he not been disconcertingly honest. The moment he made it known that the Pentateuch was not the work of a single author, but was compiled from different sources over a considerable period of time, his days in the chair of Hebrew and Semitic languages were numbered. MacLeod Campbell would no doubt have retired peacefully in the parish of Rhu had he not taught a new understanding of the doctrine of the atonement. The truth faithfully pursued and honestly expounded is bound to be costly. The spelling out of the practical implications of the Christian doctrines of the Fatherhood of God and the brotherhood of man vis-à-vis racialism and economic exploitation, inevitably issues in hostility. It leads to some kind of crucifixion. Dietrich Bonhoeffer and Martin Luther King are there to remind us of the offence inherent in honest and courageous teaching.

In addition to all this there is the pedagogical problem. Few people are born teachers and effective communication is a desperately difficult business. I have heard headmasters say that the reason so many parish ministers fail to make an impact on schools is not because they do not know their stuff, but because they lack teaching technique. The little preaching practice that is possible within the theological curriculum, dominated as it is at the moment by the degree syndrome, is on the whole divorced from teaching. The average sermon is a stranger to any pedagogical structure. But if the content of the Christian truth is important, its communication is equally important. It may not be practicable to subject ministers to the kind of method-training teachers undergo in our colleges of education but, somewhere along the line, it must be brought home to them that a Church that despises the teaching ministry is digging its own grave.

It goes without saying that the content of the Christian message is of immense importance. There is a profound sense in which this question comes first. There is not much point in securing modern, centrally-heated, beautifully furnished classrooms, the most up-to-date media of communication, the latest technological helps, if at the end of the day the teachers are hopelessly vague as to what the basic message is. It is essential to have a firm and unambiguous grasp of what the core of the Christian faith is. McLuhan may have been deliberately exaggerating. When he claimed that the medium was the message he may have been trying to shock us out of our complacency in an electronic age. But for the Church the message is primary. The good news of the Gospel of Christ has been entrusted to her and she has been commissioned to declare it unto the whole earth.

It is because the message is basic, that its communication is of paramount importance. Traditionally, universities and centres of learning have been inclined to subordinate the communication of truth to the recognition of truth. They felt that if the truth was discovered after long and painstaking research and recognised by discerning minds, its transmission was a matter of secondary importance. This is not only a false but a dangerous dichotomy. Jesus attached infinite importance to the truth. He died for it. At the same time through the medium of his parables he proved himself a master of communication. The common people heard him gladly. The discovery of penicillin was a scientific truth of the first importance, so much so that making it available to those in need was a matter of supreme urgency. If the Church has the message which is for the healing of the nations, she must master every possible means to communicate it to those who in the deep places of their being have experienced what Kirkegaard calls the sickness unto death.

It is of supreme importance to stress the essential unity of preaching and teaching. This emphasis is evident in the Old Testament. The prophet proclaimed 'Thus saith the Lord' and called the nation to repentance. The teacher was commissioned to impart and interpret the knowledge of God in every home and in every street. In the New Testament it is not possible to draw a sharp line of distinction between preaching and teaching. Jesus was a prophet who shocked his contemporaries but he was also a patient teacher and a brilliant communicator. In the primitive Church the same tradition was apparent. Referring to the apostles the book of Acts says, 'They ceased not to teach and to preach Jesus Christ'. And it was the self-same Gospel that they preached and taught.

Preaching and teaching can be distinguished but it is unwise to draw the division between them too sharply. Professor C. H. Dodd is guilty of this in stressing too strongly the dichotomy between kerygma and didache. In his book *Apostolic Preaching and its Developments* he writes, 'The New Testament writers draw a clear distinction between preaching and teaching. The distinction is preserved alike in Gospels, Acts, Epistles and Apocalypse and must be considered characteristic of early Christian usage in general. Teaching (didache) is in a large majority of cases ethical instruction. Occasionally it seems to include what we should call apologetic, that is, the reasoned commendation of Christianity to persons interested, but not yet convinced. Sometimes, especially in the Johannine writings, it includes the exposition of theological doctrine. Preaching on the other hand, is the public proclamation of Christianity to the non-Christian world'.

As a protest against the insipid moralism which so often passes for Christianity, Dodd may have rendered valuable service. But in claiming that teaching in the early Church was largely confined to ethical instruction he has done violence to the tradition of both the Old and New Testaments. When the Church puts teaching before preaching, it inevitably becomes moralistic and legalistic. This happened in Rabbinic Judaism, and it has also happened in some expressions of Protestantism. Those who equate salvation and information have not even begun to understand the message of the New Testament.

Preaching and teaching can be distinguished but they cannot be separated. Kerygma may stand closer to revelation and didache to reason but neither can exist in a disembodied state. Revelation may defy rational analysis, but it has never ignored the humanity of the recipient or the cultural context in which the disclosure takes place. The Word of God is heard through the word of man. The unity that exists between revelation and reason must also express itself in the relation between preaching and teaching. One might even compare this essential unity with the Incarnation. The Word of God became flesh. Preaching, which is the proclamation of the Word, must not despise the flesh, which is real life, the human situation where questions are asked and decisions have to be made.

8. SIGNPOSTS IN MORAL EDUCATION

That we are living in a permissive age is a sentiment so relentlessly reiterated that it has become a hackneyed threadbare platitude. This seems to imply that morally speaking anything is allowed. The signposts that guided previous generations along the paths of right and wrong are no longer there. The moral landmarks of centuries have been obliterated. The traditional authorities that once commanded universal respect—Bible, Church, University—are not only openly questioned but even attacked with passionate intensity. In short, Christians and secularists speaking from very different presuppositions are persuaded that the times we are living in are morally speaking chaotic.

The question is whether this prevalent assumption can stand up to intelligent scrutiny. It could be cogently argued that the last century was far more permissive than the twentieth. The Victorians, a byword for their moral rectitude, permitted all sorts of injustices and brutalities. The forcing of the opium war on China was not one of the most creditable chapters in our history. The disturbing thing is that those responsible for such a policy and the millions who connived at it, ostensibly led sober and godly lives. Or consider another episode of our national history, surely one of the most sordid, the Highland clearances. Thousands of men, women and children were evicted from home and croft at short notice. The factor, Patrick Sellar on his white horse, delivering summonses in the name of the law, was more ruthless than any Stalinist Commissar. The landed gentry had discovered that sheep paid better than men. Not only did the Government of the day permit this callous programme, but the established Church, by its connivance, aided and abetted this crime against humanity.

These by no means exhaust the grim catalogue of Victorian iniquities. They colonised as if they had a divine right to subject 'the lesser breed' to perpetual servitude. They annexed territories which were not able to defend themselves. David Livingstone was appalled by what he discovered in darkest Africa. What infuriated him was not so much the fact that white people shamelessly exploited natives, but the spectacle of Christians, even missionaries, assuming a role of spurious neutrality. Furthermore the Victorian age treated criminals with the utmost ferocity. Our prisons were hell-holes—a disgrace to any country that dared to call itself civilised. The sort of social conscience that allowed children to work long hours down mines and women to die prematurely, was mercilessly exposed by none other than Charles Dickens. When Trade Unionism first came into existence, its leaders were regarded as criminals and deported to Australia. Lord Melbourne, Queen Victoria's favourite prime minister, permitted this injustice with the full approval of her strait-laced Majesty.

This kind of inhumanity would not be tolerated today. The brutal exploitation of underprivileged people is no longer accepted as belonging to the nature of things. The downtrodden and the disinherited of the earth evoke universal sympathy. Victorians sent gun-boats up the Nile, sabred dervishes at Omdurman, bayoneted sepoys in India, and were unbelievably insensitive to their own unemployed. Not so any more. Apartheid wherever it is practised arouses world-wide indignation. Captains of industry dare no longer indulge in indiscriminate sackings. They are held accountable in a way which was not even conceivable in the last century. What it all adds up to is that the Victorians, despite their vaunted puritanism, were much more permissive than our dishevelled pop generation.

But what precisely do we mean by morality? What areas of life is the word supposed to cover? The popular use of the word tends to restrict its use to the sphere of private relationships, especially that of sex. If we confine morality to the more intimate experiences of life we could concede that ours is a rather loose generation. In all probability we are worse than the Victorians, making the most liberal allowance for their secretiveness and hypocrisy. Behind the façade of respectability a great deal went on which was not published in the Victorian equivalents of the *News of the World*, and the American magazine *Playboy*.

Indeed where sex *mores* are concerned, there is a sense in which we are worse than the eighteenth century, widely regarded as the most lascivious of all ages. Boswell's *Journal* demonstrates that culture could go hand in hand with sexual depravity. In this respect Boswell, by his own admission, was a moral rake. There is a well-known argument which runs something like this. The eighteenth century was shockingly immoral, but a puritanical reaction set in in the nineteenth. Therefore, despite the extravagancies and indisciplines of our generation, we can be reasonably certain of the swing of the moral pendulum. There are those who even believe that its harbingers have already appeared among us in the shape of Muggeridge and Macdonald of *The New Yorker*.

It would be wrong to press the parallelism too far. A moral rake like Boswell, after each orgy, suffered the agonies of the damned. He experienced excruciating torments of conscience. Why? Because Boswell, however immoral his conduct, never questioned the fact that he lived in a moral universe. His own behaviour might not be exemplary but it did not occur to him to doubt the existence of independent moral imperatives. The situation today is very different. Moral relativism has taken over. Philosophers, psychologists and sociologists proclaim it as a creed, and it has become part of the mental outfit of the ordinary man. He slides out from under every challenge with the glib retort, that what is right for you is not necessarily right for him. It depends on circumstances, on his glands or those of his grandmother.

This paradox which clamours for explanation is intriguing in the extreme. In the realm of sex chaos seems to reign. Relativism is king. But in the realm of social morality the standards are more exacting than ever before. In sex relationships the modern conscience seems to be slack, even atrophied. But where social issues are concerned the contemporary conscience is sharper, more insistent and more imperious than ever before. Bertrand Russell embodies this puzzling paradox. In sex relationships he was the apostle of freedom and experimentation. He is portrayed as a sex-obsessed mathematician in Aldous Huxley's novel *The Genius and the Goddess*. The hero is a man who made original contributions to science yet could exercise no control over his own libido. But this is not the whole truth about Bertrand Russell. During the First World War, he was prepared to lose his job as a professor and go to prison for conscience's sake. On cultural, social and political issues, no modern philosopher has been so involved as Russell. In the interests of society he was prepared to risk his reputation as one of the greatest thinkers of the century. He was even prepared to make a fool of himself in being manhandled by muscular policemen in sit-down demonstrations in Trafalgar Square. We do not even begin to understand the contemporary moral crisis till we develop an awareness to this paradox— the flaccid conscience towards sex which goes hand in hand with a stringent one towards society.

But in this ambiguity, in this relativistic morass, in this chaos of values, what if any is the Christian attitude? Can the Church, through its theologians and ministers offer any guidance which will help the puzzled masses and in particular, perplexed youth to walk in the way they should go. There are the advocates of the Roman Catholic Natural Law. This theory teaches that there are a number of valid moral principles, imbedded as it were in the very constitution of things. From these we can proceed to particular demands by means of a rational process. For many this ethic is attractive because it provides a solid framework of rules and a welcome note of authority in the midst of speculative moral relativism. Such an emphasis is not likely to commend itself to the contemporary secular conscience. The doctrine of Natural Law as expounded by Catholic theologians has on the whole proved to be clumsy and unwieldy. It has not been conspicuously successful when applied to the problem of contraception.

What characterises modern Western man, Protestant, Catholic, Jewish or secular, is his autonomy. He is not bound by his past. Where his values and his place in the scheme of things are concerned, he is not a passive helpless recipient of an absolutist tradition. Modern man is free from any particular set of values imposed on him by Church or community. For him there are no given historical absolutes. In this sense he has come of age and is autonomous in a radically new way.

We inhabit a world in which darkness covers the earth, and nobody knows where the sun is going to rise, a world where the clocks are all telling a different time, where people dread the future, have no time for the past, and wear a mask to see as little as possible of the present. What then are the insights which Christian ethics offer us at a time when all the traditional certainties seem to have dissolved. We look in vain for facile prescriptions, or for straightforward 'yes' and 'no' answers, on issues of maddening complexity. At the risk of over-simplifying a question for which there is no easy answer, we can point to three insights which affect our whole understanding of Christian ethics today.

(1) *The Importance of Each Situation*
The name of Professor Joseph Fletcher is closely associated with this school of thought, but there are a number of other writers, including Bishop John Robinson, who strongly support him. The sponsors of situational or contextual ethics are inclined to encourage 'a practical temper'. They refuse to absolutise and they are suspicious of large scale generalisations. Any judgment we make must be based on accurate knowledge. It is imperative that we familiarise ourselves

with all the factors that belong to the situation under discussion. The temptation to apply rules mechanically must be resisted at all costs. The particularities and peculiarities related to the persons concerned must be studied with meticulous care.

In Edinburgh I know a man who for many years had to nurse a psychotic wife. On a number of occasions she had attempted suicide and was bitterly disappointed that her husband had always managed to get her to hospital in time. One night after working overtime he came home to find her unconscious from the effects of an overdose of barbiturates. There was a silk stocking round her neck, and a note scribbled in pencil, lying on the pillow beside her. It read 'John you know how much I have suffered. If you still love me tighten the stocking, it won't need much pressure'. He did and then rang the police. The judge, a humane imaginative man, sentenced him to six months' imprisonment, and reprimanded the hospital for letting the woman home after her last suicide attempt.

In most circumstances it is morally wrong to steal, but it is arguable that a situation may arise when theft may be even commendable. In Stalag Luft 3, the celebrated prison camp in Germany, the Gestapo carried out periodic raids in search of an underground radio. During one such raid, I managed to steal a screwdriver which one of the Gestapo thugs had dropped. I remember being inordinately proud when I handed my ill-gotten gain over to the security officer. In such a situation it was easy to accept the temporary suspension of moral principles, binding in more normal times.

It is precisely because circumstances alter cases that the situation is so very important. From this it follows that the homosexual must never be condemned just because he is different. The divorcee must not be dismissed in a cruel and cavalier manner. The circumstances in which the marriage broke down must be taken into consideration, as well as the conduct of the spouse. Before we pass judgment on a criminal, we must carefully study the pressures that pushed him into anti-social behaviour. When we ourselves make decisions many questions must be asked. How will our words and actions affect other people? Will they hurt them, destroy them, or enable them to cope more effectively with life? In other words, the situational factors are of tremendous importance in any course of action. It is arguable that the morality which takes each situation seriously, is more difficult and certainly more responsible, than the more traditional systems of morality which took refuge in rules that were automatically and universally applied.

(2) *The Pre-eminence of Persons*

This emphasis in Christian ethics is by no means new. It was none other than Jesus himself who made this a crucial issue in his ministry. The Pharisees were guilty of investing their rules with an absoluteness which destroyed any person who questioned them. And nowhere was this more evident than in their attitude to the sabbath. It is significant that it was on this issue that Jesus decided to enter into a head on collision with the establishment of his day. 'The sabbath was made for man, not man for the sabbath' he announced in the teeth of savage opposition. And thus, defying the most sacrosanct of Jewish prohibitions, he proceeded to heal on the sabbath day.

In that memorable saying what Jesus is really saying is that persons are more important than principles. The man who insists he is acting on principle and boasts about it, is invariably insensitive to others. Many of the major tragedies of history have stemmed from our failure to take this great saying of Jesus seriously. To begin with the Reformation was a genuine revolt against the authoritarianism of the medieval Church. But within a few generations the liberating movement became more concerned with principles of orthodoxy than with persons of flesh and blood. The same propensity is as endemic in politics as in religion. At first Communism was passionately interested in the disinherited masses as people who really suffered. This humanity was short-lived. After the Czars went out, the Commissars came in. Principles took precedence over persons. We are not likely to progress very far in medicine, in education, or in trade union negotiations, till we grasp the all important fact that principles are subordinate to persons. In Christian Ethics the pre-eminence of the person is bound up with the infinite value Jesus attached to the individual. The story is told of Muretus the itinerant medieval scholar, who fell ill in Lombardy and was taken to a pauper's hospital. Taking him for a tramp, the surgeons said to each other in Latin, the tongue of the learned, 'Let us experiment on this vile fellow'. Whereupon the bundle of rags on the operating table answered also in Latin 'Dare you call vile someone for whom Christ did not disdain to die'. This emphasis belongs to the very heart of the Christian faith.

(3) *The Primacy of Love*

The old morality was guilty of over-emphasising rules and regulations in controlling human behaviour. A man was moral as he was obedient to the code or to the rule book. While not dismissing this aspect altogether, the new morality places the emphasis elsewhere, namely on love. The thesis advanced is that love is the only real good. This is what Reinhold Niebuhr meant when he said 'You can't be moral if you are too strictly moral'. Morality cannot be separated from love and understanding. In the Sermon on the Mount, Jesus did not disregard law but his accent from beginning to end was on love. Rules are permissible and indeed welcome in so far as they serve persons. The new morality with its emphasis on love is not pursuing a new fad, but going back to the *fons et origo* of Christian ethics.

Critics of the new morality draw attention to the ambiguity surrounding the word love in the English language. It is used in an infinite number of contexts and there are those who question the wisdom of pinning morality to a word that can be interpreted in so many different ways. Professor Fletcher acknowledges this ambiguity but insists on retaining it

because 'the word is too rich—to throw it away ruthlessly'.
The new moralists know that love is not an infallible guide
since the persons who love are never perfect. Yet they hold
tenaciously to the supremacy of love, for it includes a
radical trust, basic to morality. To love someone is to see
things in him which would remain unseen without love. A
moral code might be more specific, but it would lack the
distinctive clairvoyant quality of love.

The secular humanist may have no difficulty in accepting
these three insights. He does not question the need for
morality but would argue that the secular basis for morality
is the need for man, individually and socially, to develop.
All human activity, from riding a bicycle to composing a
symphony, is a compound of spontaneity and self control. So
argues a scientific humanist like Waddington. Discipline,
restraint, even sacrifice, play an important part in the
evolution of the race, and in the dynamic process of fulfilment.

With much of this Christians would agree. Christian ethics
and Humanist ethics have much in common. Like Bertrand
Russell, the atheist, and Lord Soper, the Christian, they can
work together to combat evil and inequality. Humanism at
its best pays more than lip service to the doctrine of the
brotherhood of man. It has produced its prophets and its
martyrs and its apostles are prepared to fight injustice
wherever they meet it. While disavowing any belief in an
ultimate purpose they are ready to die for the truth in what
to them is an absurd and meaningless world. Christian ethics
and Humanist ethics can indeed collaborate to uphold the
dignity of man and promote his well being, but they differ
in two very important respects.

Christian ethics possesses an eschatological dimension.
Humanists speak of self-realisation, but self-conscious striving
after such an ideal is stultifying and self-defeating. In order
to fulfil our potential as individuals and communities we
need an apprehension of God, who calls us to responsible
action in the world. The God Jesus disclosed gives eschato-

logical as well as ultimate meaning, even to the tragic events for which we are held accountable. Moral health demands an awareness of a dimension of transcendence in human existence, a dimension that judges and redeems us at one and the same time.

The other respect in which Christian ethics is distinguished from Humanist ethics is on the question of grace. Erich Fromm defines humanism as 'the belief in the unity of the human race and man's potential to perfect himself by his own efforts'. While Christians in no way encourage a life of complacent inactivity, they hold that the life of faith is a response which has seized man and shaken him to his inner depth in Jesus Christ. This grace reveals to him a self and a potential which would otherwise remain hidden and un-realised. This is what Richard Niebuhr means when he says man is not so much the maker as the responder. He is 'man the answerer, man engaged in dialogue, man acting in response to action upon him'. In order to be surprised by joy after the manner of C. S. Lewis, our own small meanings must be caught up into an ultimate network of meaning. When we become aware of a security that undergirds our own fragile and ambiguous existence, and of a certainty that the void is really conquered, then we are recipients of Grace, the Gift which theologians, mystics and masters of the spiritual life, have always attributed to God.

9. STRATEGIES OF RELIGIOUS EDUCATION

On all sides there are pundits who claim that the acids of contemporary secular culture have eaten away the vitals of traditional religion. If God is dead in our day, how can we indefinitely postpone the disappearance of Faculties of Divinity and Departments of Religion. To many educationists, religion is no more than another mythology, useful in times past for psychological sanity and social cohesion, but for 'man come of age' no longer necessary. In a culture dominated by humanistic ideals and an all-conquering technology, religion seems to be reduced to the level of a pathetic anachronism, a tool in the hands of cynical rulers, a drug for a few lonely and nostalgic souls.

It can also be argued that the cultural climate is becoming more hospitable to the inclusion of religious studies in centres of education where the basic presuppositions are predominantly secular. When the secular/sacred dichotomy is pressed too far, when the place where the dimension of the ultimate normally resides is left vacant, the demonic takes possession, just as the parable teaches. Sooner or later, as Russia, Germany and the USA so tragically illustrate, advanced technical societes, proudly parading their secularity, espouse the demonic myths of race and class and nation. If man is naturally religious, a fact which the evidence of history seems to corroborate, the dimension of ultimacy in his life cannot be ignored. Religion in all its richness, creative powers and infinite variety must become an object of academic study.

Someone writing about the late Thurber of *The New Yorker* said that he had a clear grasp of confusion. This perhaps should be our modest ambition for religious educa-

91

tion in school and church. In both contexts confusion abounds. Historically, even in countries where the teaching of religion in schools is compulsory, its low status in the curriculum has precluded serious treatment. Philosophically there has been lack of clarity as to how religion can be integrated within a general scheme of education. For this exceedingly complex problem there is no glib formula. Perhaps all we can hope for at this stage is a Thurberesque strategy of grasping as clearly as possible the ambiguity which in fact exists.

The strategy we employ in religious education within school and university is bound to be different from the one we employ within the Church. The presuppositions of our educational institutions are predominantly secular, while those of our ecclesiastical institutions are not necessarily so. This of course does not imply that the Church is a citadel of faith, standing impregnable and intact, untouched by any kind of secular influence. Because the Church is a human as well as a divine institution, no neat demarcation between sacred and secular can be drawn. The truth is that there is a celebration of the secular going on, not only outside but also inside the Church. This movement we associate with names like Harvey Cox, Dr John Robinson and Ronald Gregor Smith. But long before these writers became known as apostles of the secular, Bonhoeffer, not in a book-lined study, but in one of the cells of Tegel prison, had joyfully celebrated 'the worldliness of Christianity'.

(1) *Religious Education within a Secular Context*

It is possible to put up a fairly strong case for the inclusion of religious education within the general educational curriculum on the basis of socio-cultural understanding alone. How can anyone who is not helplessly prejudiced deny the importance of religion in human history and culture? It would be crassly absurd to talk of European culture without giving students some sort of appreciation of the role religion has played in the past and still does. How can an honest teacher do justice to the sixteenth century if he does not draw attention to the influence of religious figures like Martin Luther and John Calvin. Indeed, a good argument can be advanced for the study of Church history in our secondary schools on the ground that up to the Reformation and for some time after, secular history is incomprehensible without it. I believe the Germans have already introduced such a course. In brief, because religion is an important cultural phenomenon, it ought to become a major concern of general education. It should be taught in order to promote cultural and historical awareness.

Again we can defend the inclusion of religious studies within the general scheme of education on the ground that it is possible to distinguish between the teaching *of* religion and the teaching *about* religion. Teaching about religion is predominantly informative, not evangelistic in its aim. Its goal is not to compel decision but to convey facts. For example, instead of asking for a confession that Jesus Christ is Lord, it teaches that from the beginning 'Christos Kurios'—Christ is Lord—was a central notion of the Christian faith. Presumably because it does not insist on personal commitment, the latter approach ensures a greater degree of objectivity. If this is what we mean by religious education, there is no reason in the world why an honest humanist could not teach religion every bit as effectively as the most committed Christian.

But this distinction cannot be pushed too far. It does not follow that personal commitment and the honest presentation of a subject are mutually exclusive. It is possible for one astronomer to support the 'big bang' theory of the origin of the universe, for another to espouse the 'steady state' theory, and for yet another to be absolutely neutral in this regard. It would be wrong, however, to question an astronomer's adequacy to teach the subject on the basis of such commitments. The proper way to judge his competency as a teacher would be on the basis of his knowledge, and his ability to subject astronomical theory to critical examination. Provided this is done sensitively and openly the learner's vision is enlarged and his experience immeasurably enriched.

In his *Secular Education and the Logic of Religion* Professor Ninian Smart develops an argument which appeals to me greatly. Drawing our attention to the existing schizophrenia in religious education, the dichotomy between indoctrination on the one hand, and the mere transmission of information on the other, Smart pleads for a more imaginative and creative approach. Many Humanists and indeed some liberally minded Christians object to the school or university being taken over as evangelistic platforms, where captive audiences are bludgeoned into submission. But equating religion with the historical is not much more satisfactory. The transmission of dry as dust information about ancient documents and venerated scrolls is not likely to galvanise bored students into transports of enthusiasm for the subject. It is far more likely to increase their disenchantment with all things religious.

Professor Smart goes on to argue that the inherent, inner logic of theology forces it outward into the study of philosophy, sociology, comparative religions, ethics, etc. In other words there is a descriptive, historical side to religion which the most truculent agnostic is bound to acknowledge. But there is also a para-historical side to religion, and to separate these two dimensions is to do violence to the integrity of the subject. Religion is a multi-dimensional phenomenon and all the dimensions are mutually dependant. They constitute a unity in plurality. Religious education taken seriously must transcend the merely informative. Part of the job is to initiate students not just into knowledge of the written records, but also into the meaning and truth of religion. According to Ian Ramsey, the purpose of religious education is 'to teach insight, to evoke disclosures in which we come to ourselves when and as we discern a world which has "come alive" in some particular situation.' What Christian education in particular seeks to do is to create this response and this fulness of life—this commitment—in relation to a discernment which occurs around the person of Jesus Christ, as discovered in the Bible, in doctrine and in worship.

Space forbids more than a mere mention of one of the most vexing problems of religious education, namely language. In reading the Bible no one can fail to be impressed by the sharpness, and appositeness of the models used. In those far-off days, when men living in an agrarian community were daily exposed to military assault, shepherd, fortress and shield were appropriate symbols of a sublime trust in an over-arching Providence. In today's world, social security may be more meaningful than shield, and a personnel officer than the good shepherd. 'God is my co-pilot' may sound blasphemously trite in comparison with 'The Lord is my Shepherd', but the use of such a model, inadequate though it is, illustrates the need for models that speak meaningfully to a generation born and nurtured by a society dominated by technology.

The Report on *Moral and Religious Education in Schools* by the commission appointed a number of years ago by the Secretary of State for Scotland, is sensitive to all the problems I have mentioned, but the recommendations seem to me to be over-cautious and distinctly timid. To argue that making Religious Education examinable would reduce the importance of the subject is, to say the least of it, odd. It smacks of Rousseaunian idealism, blind to the ambitious perversity of human nature. I myself would favour a double-barrelled approach. The study of religion in the historical socio-cultural sense should be compulsory for all pupils in our secondary schools, once qualified teachers are available. At the same time as many students as possible should be encouraged to take Religious Education on an Ordinary or Higher level, on the understanding that its status was as good as English or mathematics for the purpose of qualifying for university entrance.

(2) *Religious Education within a Church Context*
The Christian faith is centred on a belief in a Sovereign God,

who acts in history. One of his most significant actions was to call a people to obey him and be the instruments of his invincible purpose. The Old Testament is the record and interpretation of these mighty acts: Exodus, Deliverance from Egypt and Covenant. In the New Testament, the followers of Jesus thought of themselves as the New Israel. But if they were conscious of their continuity with the people of God in the Old Testament, they were even more conscious of their discontinuity. Both the Old and New Testaments regard the induction of children into knowledge of God's acts, as belonging to the very nature of the Church. Deuteronomy enjoins parents and teachers that total commitment to monotheism be taught to their children. And in Ephesians, fathers are exhorted not to provoke their children to wrath but 'to bring them up in the nurture and admonition of the Lord'.

In any discussion of Religious Education we cannot evade the question of the original purpose. It seems that Jesus, though he did not draw a rigid distinction between preaching and teaching, practised the latter in intimate person-to-person situations. It was not enough to respond once and for all to the call 'Repent for the Kingdom of God is at hand'. The first fine careless rapture of faith could so easily turn into a new Pharisaic self-confidence. So over and over again, by means of parable and allegory he taught his disciples the meaning of faith. They had to be instructed more fully in the truth, in order that they might shed their inadequate understanding of God. All this led up to the basic strategy Jesus was mapping out for his followers. They were disciples so that later they could become apostles. They were being trained to exercise the Ministry Jesus began, with increasing power and breadth: 'Greater works than these shall ye do'.

If asked what Religious Education within a Church context is about, most people would automatically think of the Sunday School or the Bible Class, so from the beginning we are plagued with the confusion of more or less identifying education with a particular agent. In the USA a great deal of research has been put in on the Sunday School. The findings are on the whole depressing. In his book *Big Little School* Robert Lynn argues that the Sunday School is intimately related to nineteenth-century evangelical Protestantism. Where the evangelical spirit is alive today, provided it is supported by cult-like congregations, the Sunday School prospers. Where the evangelical spirit is in decline as in the main line denominations, the Sunday School is in disarray. In America the importance attached to Religious Education since the First World War seems to be grotesquely ineffective. In Britain the average church attendance is little more than 10 per cent of the population. In the USA it is 43 per cent, yet in a survey which asked people to name the four Gospels, 61 per cent in Britain answered correctly against 35 per cent in the USA. No doubt a whole host of other factors must be considered, but this mass ignorance would seem to indicate that directors of Religious Education, the expenditure of vast sums of money on curricula, programmes, and electronic means of communication are no guarantee of theological literacy.

I would agree with Dr John Gray of Edinburgh University, that the fact of diminishing numbers at public worship is no reason for abandoning the Sunday School. It should be looked on as one means among others for training children in the nurture and admonition of the Lord. And with Dr Gray I would emphasise the importance of exposing the curriculum planners and teachers to the researches of men like Piaget and Goldman. Piaget argues that there are three different kinds of thinking. The first is what he calls pre-operational and is characteristic of children up to the age of seven. The second stage he describes as operational or concrete and covers the years approximately from seven to eleven. The third stage marked by a capacity for abstract thinking is not reached till about the age of thirteen. In his *Religious Thinking from Childhood to Adolescence* Goldman's indebtedness to Piaget is abundantly clear. The three different stages Piaget differentiates, Goldman describes as intuitive, concrete and abstract. On the basis of his researches extending over many years, he stresses the necessity for teaching religion to younger juniors by means of life themes like 'Our Homes', 'People who help us', 'Shepherds and their Sheep'.

The insights of men like Piaget and Goldman are invaluable for Religious Education. This is so even if we cannot completely agree with their assessment of the successive stages in a child's thinking. My first reaction in reading Piaget, many years ago, was to question his argument that abstract thinking begins at the age of twelve or thirteen. In the Hebrides, where children were brought up on the shorter catechism in two languages, I am almost certain that the capacity for conceptual thought began much earlier. Hence my excitement when recently a number of Oxford Dons, on the basis of much wider sampling, claim that Piaget was wrong and that children are capable of abstract thinking at a much earlier age.

Using the insights of Piaget and others, we have to use some system of grading in order to communicate the Bible meaningfully to children. There is no point in bombarding them with stories and texts if they do not understand them. For example the story of Abraham leaving Ur of the Chaldees, with no cast-iron certainties, or gilt-edged securities, is meaningful for adults and teenagers. It speaks to the human capacity for adventure and exploration. To a child, the story of Abraham can be a terrifying experience. At this stage separation from home and parents is unthinkable. But grading is not the same thing as distortion. It simply means that we respect the mental development of a child and show some sensitivity to what, at a particular age, he is capable of absorbing. The whole purpose of scripture teaching is to induct children into faith in the living God. The quantitative is therefore irrelevant. One passage, one story, one character, sensitively expounded, may open up the way to faith, while a hundred chapters, not geared to the child's age, can only engender confusion.

Christian education must not be confined to Sunday School or Junior Bible Class. Someone once remarked with great perception that Christ taught adults and played with children, while we in our churches today teach children and play with adults. The adults themselves must accept a major share of responsibility for this anomaly. Not one out of ten of those who attend church has any intention of engaging in serious study or serious learning. They come to public worship looking for comfort, inspiration, enjoyment, not for an increase of knowledge and wisdom. Ministers on the whole have been too accommodating. Too timid in their exposition of the Bible, they take refuge in moralising and dishonest allegorising and Church members become progressively more illiterate.

The question we have to examine is what Church education is about. There are those who would say that the particular role of religious education within a Church setting is to help develop a Christian mentality. This answer is good enough as far as it goes, provided we resist the temptation of over-intellectualising the educational content. Christian education, properly understood, must reach down into the deep springs of a person's life, the springs of motivation and commitment. What the Church needs desperately at the moment is a spiritual dynamic allied with educational effectiveness. An evangelical emphasis can very easily move in the direction of pietism and obscurantism, but properly understood it is not at all incompatible with intellectual reflection and the promotion of just social policies.

From this it follows that the teacher of religion, whatever the particular setting—pulpit, kirk session, adolescent groups, or Sunday School—must be adequately trained. He must have some theological understanding of the material he is supposed to impart, and he must master as best he can the latest techniques of communication. It is significant that right across the world there is a revival of interest in the quality of Christian education. In Canada and America 'Church School' teachers are expected to undergo a fairly exacting training course. In Scotland, according to a report published in 1960, it was estimated that less than one-third of our Sunday School teachers had received any training. Since then steps have been taken to rectify this serious omission. Credit for this progress goes to the Committee on the Religious Instruction of Youth. The Committee bases its tactics on the sound assumption that at a time of ferment, and seismic cultural upheaval, Christian Education demands the keenest minds and the liveliest spirits in the Church.

BIOGRAPHICAL AND BIBLIOGRAPHICAL NOTES TO PART THREE: THE MINISTER AS TEACHER

7. CINDERELLA STATUS OF THE TEACHING MINISTRY

Robertson Smith
Professor of Hebrew in the Free Church College, Aberdeen. In a celebrated heresy trial he was deposed by the Free Church General Assembly. His most famous book is *The Religion of the Semitics* on which Freud leant rather heavily.

MacLeod Campbell
Minister of the parish of Rhu, Dunbartonshire. In 1831, after an acrimonious trial, he was deposed by the General Assembly of the Church of Scotland. His theology of the atonement clashed with the rigid Calvinist orthodoxy of his day. According to Professor H. R. MacIntosh he was our greatest Scottish theologian. Author of *The Nature of the Atonement*.

C. H. Dodd
Emeritus Professor of New Testament in Cambridge. His name has been associated with 'Realised Eschatology'. Author of over twenty books, among them *Parables of the Kingdom*, *The Apostolic Preaching and its Development* and *The Founder of Christianity*. He was also Joint Director of the translation of the New English Bible.

8. SIGNPOSTS IN MORAL EDUCATION

Patrick Sellar
The notorious factor who on his white horse rode around the villages of Sutherland, delivering summonses of eviction to crofters.

Joseph Fletcher
Professor of Social Ethics at Harvard, USA. His name is associated with situation ethics. Fletcher does not insist on scrapping rules, only on subordinating rules to love. He describes his approach as personalistic and contextual. His best-known work is *Situation Ethics*.

Erich Fromm
A post-Freudian psychologist. More than most psychologists he stresses the importance of society in the shaping of personality. While many contemporary psychologists are apostles of moral relativism, Fromm stresses the importance of morality. His best-known works are *Man for Himself*, *The Fear of Freedom*, *The Sane Society*.

9. STRATEGIES OF RELIGIOUS EDUCATION

Jean Piaget
A Swiss psychologist who carried out experiments on the thought development of children. He has exercised a strong influence in child psychology, and has made solid contributions to our understanding of Religious Education. One of his best-known works is *The Language and Thought of the Child*.

Ronald Goldman
An English psychologist whose experiments in Religious Education are more extensive than those of Piaget. In giving a systematic account of religious thinking from six to seventeen years he adds a new dimension to our insights into child and adolescent development. His best-known books are *Religious Thinking from Childhood to Adolescence* and *Readiness for Religion*.

Ronald Gregor Smith
The late Professor of Divinity in Glasgow University who was one
of the first English-speaking theologians to take the secular
dimension of our life seriously. His best-known works are *The
New Man* and *Secular Christianity*.

Harvey Cox
Professor of Theology and Culture at Andover Newton Theological School, USA. He shows a special interest in secularisation
and urbanisation. He argues that the new freedom of contemporary man demands a larger measure of maturity and
responsibility. His best-known work is *The Secular City*.

Part Four

THE MINISTER AS PASTOR

10. IMPORTANCE OF PSYCHOTHERAPY

Sigmund Freud was one of the truly great revolutionaries who changed the attitudes and to a considerable degree influenced the conduct of mankind. As an original thinker he can take his place with Copernicus and Darwin. An authentic genius, he was courageous enough to question the most rigid orthodoxies and sacrosanct traditions of his day, and to usher in a new era of ferment and unrest. In the teeth of opposition from his own profession, and vilification from the academic world he tenaciously adhered to his convictions. These he proclaimed through books, lectures, interviews and the celebrated clinic he established in Vienna.

Basic to Freud's entire psychology was his theory of personality. He conceived of the self after the model of a family dwelling upon different floors in the same house. The family on the first floor is decent, law-abiding and utterly respectable. In the basement there lives a large family of an unruly and disreputable character. To begin with some members of the basement family belonged to the first floor, but like fallen angels they were pushed downstairs. The occupants of the basement are selfish and obstreperous. Their one preoccupation is the gratification of their desires which are predominantly sexual. In order to do this they are determined to push up to the first floor where they can indulge themselves much more freely. The family dwelling there, however, are equally determined to resist their efforts. In their anxiety they appoint some sort of policeman, planting him on top of the stairs to guard the approach from below.

Freud distinguished three main aspects of personality. The *Id* is the conglomeration of basic drives present at birth; the

need for food, sex and the rage which results when these
appetites are not satisfied. Gradually there develops a part
of the personality, the *Ego*, which mediates between the Id
and the outside world. The Ego has to deal with the frustrations which occur when the basic drives of personality are
baulked. It is characterised by the reality principle and is
what we normally recognise as 'I'.

The super-Ego develops from the restrictions imposed on
children by parents and adults, even more from what they
imagine to be forbidden and required. These commands and
prohibitions are incorporated in an exaggerated form to make
up what Freud calls 'the primitive unconscious conscience'.
Adults are aware of much of the Ego aspects of personality,
but not of the Id or the super-Ego except by their effects. At
times most of us have experienced anger out of all proportion
to its apparent causes, and compulsions to follow a certain
course of action against every dictate of reason.

According to Freud, the most powerful and most pervasive
of human drives are sexual. One of the most important of all
his concepts is that of the Oedipus Complex. This arises
because the child wants sole possession of its mother and sees
the father as a powerful rival. This leads to fantasies designed
to get rid of the father and being in turn punished. These
fantasies give rise to anxieties that are promptly repressed,
that is, pushed down into the depth of the unconscious where
they lurk, ready to spring on us when we relax our guard. To
change the metaphor, the various anxieties are like a stream
which is made to flow underground to form a swamp. This
swamp in the unconscious is what we mean by a complex.
In time this hidden complex may express itself in nervousness,
hysteria, neurosis and all sorts of obsessions.

These stages of psychosexual development, Freud believed,
were more or less complete at about five years of age. While
little is remembered on a conscious level, nevertheless the
relationships formed in infancy determine the child's later
relationships with other people. They are at the root of
neurotic behaviour on the one hand, or healthy adjustment

on the other, in adult life. The attitudes built up in infancy towards the parents are transferred to other people who may play a very important part in the grown-up person's life—wife, husband, boss, friends or enemies.

The Freudian method of treatment, and indeed that of other psychoanalysts who would not go all the way with Freud, requires a change in the total personality. This is attempted through the patients' relationships with the psychoanalyst. As in other relationships the patient acts towards the analyst as he once did towards his parents, hating and loving him at one and the same time. The analyst accepts this and in the process of explaining it, deepens the patient's understanding and opens up the way to more adult attitudes. A basic presupposition of psychoanalysis is that once the patient fully understands the reason lying behind his irrational behaviour, he is freed from the tyranny of his neurosis. The relationship between therapist and patient is one of mutual trust.

The Second World War gave psychoanalysis a great boost. Under its pressures, medical officers used 'front line psychiatry', makeshift forms of mental first aid, the cult of reassurance, the talking out of the soldiers' fears and the restoration of his lost confidence. While the relief this method gave was limited, nevertheless it helped victims of battle fatigue, who otherwise might have been emotionally crippled for the rest of their lives. Greatly impressed, a number of doctors after the war turned to psychiatry, believing it was the panacea for all ills. The nineteen-fifties were a high-water mark of psychiatry's influence and prestige. It became a sort of fad, so much so that words like complex, projection, obsession were bandied about by cocktail party pundits, New Left activists and law-and-order Conservatives. It was part of the fashion.

A reaction was bound to set in, and over the last decade or so, it has come with a vengeance. A profusion of articles appeared in popular and technical publications, assuring us that psychoanalysis is passé, outmoded, a quaint anachronism, a thing of the past. Professor Mowrer of America predicted it would not survive a single generation. Professor Eysenck of Britain argues in books, monographs and popular articles that psychoanalysis is a fraudulent theory and a harmful therapy which actually retards recovery.

Coinciding with, perhaps even accelerating, the decline of interest in psychoanalysis was the advent of chemotherapy—the use of drugs to help the mentally ill. It was in the mid-fifties that tranquillisers burst upon the scene and began to revolutionise the treatment of psychotics and anxious, over-wrought neurotics. The psychopharmacologists speculated that drugs inhibited excessive chemical activity in the brain and thereby modified harmful behaviour. They talked of tantalising clues of chemical imbalance in the urine of schizophrenics and even of neurotics. To those who were always suspicious of psychoanalysis it was clear that faulty chemistry was the explanation of mental illness and correct chemistry the cure.

This is tantamount to saying that insulin cures diabetes. Doctors do not know how to cure diabetics but they know how to keep diabetics alive. Similarly chemotherapy is ameliorative, not curative. How marvellous it would be if all the world's madness, sadism and inhumanity could be eliminated by means of chemistry! But though the alleged chemical cure has been heralded with trumpets, it has not turned out to be the panacea for our mental disorders. Logically there is no inherent contradiction between psychopharmacology and psychoanalysis.

Another development has been the emergence of behaviour therapy. Professor Skinner of Harvard, the well-known behaviourist-psychologist (with his rats, teaching machines and operant conditioning) and Wolpe (who has worked out techniques of behaviour therapy, applicable to human beings) start off from a firm Pavlovian position. They argue that a neurosis is not evidence of an unconscious conflict, but of a bad habit—a matter of faulty conditioning. The obsessional neurotic who retraces his steps some twenty times to make sure he has locked the door behind him, can be deconditioned. Similarly with the drug addict, claim the behaviour therapists. The cure is simple. Administer an electric shock every time he reaches for dope till the very thought of drugs fills him with repugnance.

Does this simplistic therapy really work? Wolpe and his colleagues report high cure-rates, claiming that no substitute symptoms have appeared, thus proving that there is no hidden underlying conflict. If the claim the behaviour therapists make for their approach can be substantiated, it not only disqualifies the practise of psychotherapy, but at the same time reduces counselling and pastoral care to the point of absurdity. Why ask man to exercise his divine gift of freedom, if he can be deconditioned like a rat in a maze, or a salivating dog in a kennel.

Critics of behaviour therapy claim that there are serious flaws in Wolpe's evidence. They also point out that every new therapy introduced over the last forty years has shown an exceptionally high cure-rate at first but not later. Sir William Osler used to tell his medical students that the time to use a therapy was when it was brand new. Only then does it cure nearly everyone. The other point is that the number of patients who can be treated by deconditioning techniques is rather small. It seems to lend itself more readily to people suffering from phobias and allied states. Many of the claims made for the treatment of homosexuals and alcoholics are either unreliable or unconfirmed.

In his useful paperback *New Horizons in Psychiatry* Peter Hays seems to me to strike a sane note on the subject. He pays tribute to the positive contributions of behaviour therapy in certain situations while at the same time he stresses its distinct limitations. 'It is to be hoped that the learning theory views and Freudian insights into the same dynamics may be blended into a consistent theory at some future date, a theory more scientific than Freud's and less starkly mechanistic than that evolved from Pavlov and Hull.'

Sceptics are fond of reminding theologians of the conflicting interpretations of Christianity that play havoc with a clear-cut witness in a perplexed pluralistic society. This cannot be denied, but the divisions of psychology are if anything more numerous. Freudians, Jungians, Behaviourists do not always speak with one voice and, like theologians, they have a tendency to sanctify their own particular orthodoxies. In a remarkable paper, published in the *American Journal of Psychiatry* (1969) entitled 'A Cross-National Study of Diagnosis', Morton Kramer confronts us with statistics which the ordinary layman must regard as somewhat alarming. If I were admitted to a mental hospital in England I would have ten times a higher chance of being classified as a manic depressive than if I were admitted to a hospital in the USA. On the other hand if I were to enter a mental hospital in the USA I would have a 33 per cent higher chance of being classified a schizophrenic than in Britain.

How should the minister of religion look on secular psycho-therapy? Should he approach it tentatively, regarding it more as an enemy than as an ally of the faith? According to Professor Hobart Mowrer, the American psychologist, clergymen defer far too easily to secular psychotherapists, who do not recognise the reality of guilt, only guilt feelings. Ministers of religion, Mowrer argues, provided they realised the healing resources of the Christian faith, could deal much more effectively with the emotionally disturbed than could the big guns in psychoanalysis.

Mowrer's rebuke may indeed be salutary, but we should on no account be tempted to abandon the profound insights of psychologists like Freud, Adler and Jung. Modern psychology has taught us that much of what has traditionally passed for sin was in fact a complex, a neurosis, an obsession —whatever we like to call it. Thus the severity of traditional moral standards has been reduced but by no means elim-inated. Theology will not allow us to side-step the paradox of sin. It emphasises the inevitability of human sin and the fact that man must be held responsible for it.

But what about guilt? Can there be any agreement

between the Christian minister and the secular psychologist on such a crucial question? It is important to draw a distinction between authentic guilt and pathological guilt. The Scottish soldier who unintentionally shot a German civilian in 1945, and years later confessed, was demonstrating the meaning of what I mean by 'healthy guilt'. The girl student who felt guilty every time she saw a child cross a street in case it got killed, was showing all the signs of pathological guilt. Strictly speaking normal guilt is the province of the theologian while the pathological variety is that of the psychiatrist.

The two provinces cannot be separated too neatly. At times guilt assumes neurotic forms, but among the sanest of people it expresses itself in a sense of alienation and ontological insecurity. In his *Divided Self*, R. D. Laing is surely right in pointing out that Shakespeare's scepticism was different from that of Kafka. Shakespeare was very conscious of the irrational and absurd dimensions of human existence, and expressed them in unforgettable language. Life is described as a tale told by an idiot, as the plaything of chance and accident. 'As flies to wanton boys, are we to the gods, they kill us for their sport' (*King Lear*). Nevertheless Shakespeare's characters, his captains and kings and clowns, are robust, red-blooded creatures, who know their own identity. In Kafka the situation is radically different. His characters do not know who they are. They are stripped down to an abstract humanity, and they are strangers to self identity. Long before death strikes them down, something terrible has happened to them. The Kafka character is a cipher whose existence is pointless. It is in such a situation where our human existence is marked by ontological anxiety that theology is even more relevant than psychology.

There can be no basic dichotomy between theology and psychotherapy because they are both preoccupied with healing. In the past the medical profession was inclined to limit health to physical well-being, forgetting that behind the smooth functioning of the organism lie imponderable mysteries. There are doctors who even today view psychologists with suspicion. They are inclined to describe a psychologist as one who tells you what everybody knows in a language nobody understands.

Churchmen were equally guilty of devaluing the concept of healing but in a different way. They proclaimed salvation but were apt to equate salvation with a post-mortem heaven reserved for superannuated Christians, or else with the assurance that the fortunate ones were among the elect. This view of salvation has become absolutely meaningless to the modern mind. Theologians and psychotherapists alike were guilty of the internalising of the meaning of salvation and of the discrediting of political solutions. Erich Fromm is surely right when he argues that we must work hard to create a sane society, in order to produce sane individuals.

But what do we mean by healing? Every answer we proffer seems to sell us short. They fail to do justice to the depth of the question. They change it from a dynamic human concern into a lifeless inert bundle of words. The truth is that to this basic question there aren't any answers, certainly not simplistic ones. With great insight Jung once remarked that the serious problems of life are never solved, and that if they were something very important would be lost.

In authentic religion as well as in psychotherapy, there are no smooth answers, no clear-cut solutions. In his predicament, neat formulae would leave the patient worse off than before. What we have to do is help the patient to embrace, encompass and integrate the problem. The problems must be faced in their full meaning and the contradictions accepted. They must be built upon until healing comes from a new level of consciousness.

No one discipline has a monopoly of healing. If healing means wholeness, the life more abundant, a state of well-being, then indeed many agents will help to bring this beatitude into existence. They will include politicians, psychiatrists, social workers, school teachers and ministers of religion. We must not be too arrogant to acknowledge that the resources of being truly human are not the monopoly of Church, medicine or psychotherapy. Precisely because God is creator these resources are found everywhere. Like the sense sublime Wordsworth sang about, they pervade the whole of reality. Their dwelling is the light of setting suns, the round ocean, the living air, the blue sky, the mind of man. They roll through all things.

11. THE ROLE OF THE COUNSELLOR

From time immemorial, counselling has gone on in some shape or other. The older professions have always meddled in other people's affairs with varying degrees of success. Lawyers, doctors and ministers possessed certain skills and their expertise commanded a considerable amount of respect. In addition to the authority invested in them and the mystique that surrounds their respective callings, this made them formidable figures in any community. In pre-Freudian days they may not have been over-sensitive to the delicate and complex structure we call personality but they were not without sympathy and insight. There are those who are prepared to argue that despite their authoritarian tendencies, they were on balance on the side of the angels.

It was in this present century that their authority as counsellors came to be questioned, following inevitably in the wake of the Freudian revolution. Explorations of the unconscious side of personality in clinics, sprouting all over the world, seemed to cast doubt on the 'advice giving' of the established professions. The didactic prescriptions and pointed directives of conventional wisdom were powerless to liberate those who were victims of serious emotional disturbance. They needed new insights and new motives which had to be arrived at with a certain measure of spontaneity before the miracle of release took place. It is against such a background that we can talk of the advent of the counsellors.

The aim of counselling, whatever specific label we attach to it is to enable people to cope more effectively with various stresses, and to adapt themselves with a greater degree of flexibility to situations that can be agonisingly complex. It has been defined in the following terms: 'Assisting an individual to develop insight and ability to adjust to successive events in his life, through the appraisal of his capacities, aptitudes and interests; helping him to understand motivations, emotional reactions and compensatory behaviour; and helping him to attain a degree of personal integration whereby he can most effectively use his potentialities and make the greatest contribution to the society in which he lives.'

In the USA, the term counselling has been used in a somewhat narrower sense than in Britain. It has been taken to refer to a comparatively brief number of meetings during which a professional works out a parishioner's problems. After a period of discussion, and an effort at clarification, the counselled may be referred to other agents who can help, either with more information or with more material support. In this chapter I intend to use counselling in a much more comprehensive sense. Its aim may be that of uncovering hidden motives, unmasking perverted intentions, or dragging a repressed fear into the light of day. If a disturbed person's illusions are to be taken into account, it is exceedingly difficult to draw a sharp line of distinction between counselling and psychotherapy.

The term 'counsellor' can be used to include psychiatrists, psychoanalysts, psychotherapists and social case workers. After we have made the most generous allowance for the big difference in population, the USA have three times as many counsellors as Great Britain. This numerical superiority may be explicable in terms of cultural differences, or to emotional stresses inherent in a highly competitive society, but the true explanation may simply be a higher standard of living. Affluence and counselling appear to go together. The appetite for physical amenities, which is a mark of contemporary civilisations, goes hand in hand with a desire for non-material benefits, and so the future of the counsellor seems assured. Counselling covers such a vast territory that all we can do is to discuss a number of the more important aspects.

(1) *Paradoxes of Counselling*

In his book *The Faith of the Counsellors* Paul Halmos claims that the majority of counsellors are frankly and humbly agnostic. In a pluralistic and secularised age this helps to commend him to those who are suspicious of anything smacking of piety. Yet while most counsellors are avowedly agnostic they act on presuppositions which can be interpreted as religious. Halmos is prepared to argue that the language counsellors use to express subtle and complex interpersonal relationships has a distinct theological flavour. They may vehemently deny this but as George Bernard Shaw said, we know what a man believes not from the creed he formally professes, but from the assumptions on which he habitually acts.

The counsellor believes in the worth-whileness of the patient. Those who come with their predicaments may be unattractive, even repulsive. They may be truculent, aggressive and stupidly non-co-operative. They may even be hostile and spitefully malicious. Nevertheless the counsellor is dedicated to the task of healing them. In other words, he acts in a way which can only be described as religious. This is how Halmos sums it up: 'To call this exercise an outcome of faith is, I believe well warranted for it has many of the characteristics of human experience and behaviour with which we associate the notion of faith.'

There is also the paradox of emotion and reason. From Freud onwards counsellors have proceeded on the assumption that our psychological predicaments were caused by emotional blockages located somewhere in the depth of the unconscious. These repressed fears and obsessions had to be dragged up into the light of rational scrutiny before the patient could experience the beatitude of release. Supported by his disciples, Freud did much to discredit eighteenth-century pretensions that man was basically a rational creature. On the contrary, said the psychoanalysts, man was a creature of his emotions, a plaything of blind unconscious forces, at the beck and call of basic instinctual drives. Yet paradoxically enough it was these very prophets who argued that rational insight into our own modes of behaviour was the only condition of freedom from neurotic bondage. Whether he is prepared to admit it or not, the counsellor is forced to come to terms with the paradox of the irrationality and rationality of every patient he interviews.

Yet again there is the paradox of the objective and the subjective. Counsellors who have undergone rigorous training believe in detachment. Precisely because they have been trained to adopt a scientific approach, to observe, to analyse and diagnose in the most dispassionate manner possible, they are on their guard against any attitude which could be construed as soft and sentimental. This objectivity is very important. Whether his status be amateur or professional, a counsellor should be sufficiently skilled to know whether he is dealing with a neurotic, a psychotic or a schizophrenic. But the counsellor is faced with the task not only of diagnosis, but also with that of healing. And the inescapable dilemma is this. If his aim is to rehabilitate the patient, and enable him at the end of the day to live a useful and comparatively happy life in society, can he consistently maintain this attitude of scientific objectivity? The considerable amount of literature we have on this subject, American, Continental and British, tends to give a negative answer to this question.

In practice, counsellors have discovered that if they want to be effective, they cannot separate objectivity and sympathy. No matter how scrupulously scientific they endeavour to be, they cannot prevent the empirical and the logical from getting hopelessly mixed up with the intuitive and the introspective. From many sources and from very different schools of psychotherapeutic thought it is possible to quote numerous declarations of faith in the virtue of human empathy. In other words, skill and love are not enemies, but allies in the task of healing. They are not necessarily antithetical but bound together in a mysterious paradoxical creative relationship. Erich Fromm, himself a counsellor and a trainer of counsellors writes: 'The only way of full knowledge lies in the act of love.'

To the philosopher, paradox may be anathema and may signal the end of meaningful argument, but to the mystic it is the germ of faith. On the whole, psychological literature has shown that those who show a preference for black-and-white statements are merely expressing infantile ambivalent attitudes towards their parents. This explains the behaviour of people who see every issue as either black or white, and who love or hate others without reservation. The racialist mentality, so common even in sophisticated sections of the community, can probably be traced to early childhood. No doubt the interaction of other complex forces in the environment play an important part, but the love/hate ambivalence towards parents in early infancy may constitute its inner core.

Which raises an important question. In the selection of counsellors what qualities do we look for? There is no easy answer to this problem. No system of selection, however well devised is proof against error, but a good counsellor is a person who is free of dogmatic certainties about people and causes. He is under no compulsive pressure to arrive at a clear-cut decision in every conceivable situation and he is capable of an even-tempered tolerance of inconsistencies. The counsellor does not rely entirely on intuition. He will try to acquire as much socio-psychological knowledge as he can. He knows that well-meaning kindness and uncritical loving-ness are not enough, but he also knows he is dealing with human personality, the mystery of which transcends all neat, pigeon-holed scientific categories. The good counsellor respects logic, but he is also open to the theory of 'creative dissonance'. Far from being ashamed of paradox, he accepts it as a psychological necessity in the interest of healing.

(2) *Methods of Counselling*

The most basic principle of counselling is that of acceptance. The patient may use the counsellor as a target for all his repressed hostilities, phobias and pent-up frustrations, and because he is at the receiving end he may be tempted to reciprocate. This must be strongly resisted for there is no possibility of healing till the patient knows he is not on probation, but is accepted, just as he is, torn asunder by a mass of self-deceptions and paranoic fears. Somehow or other, however unpalatable the situation may be, the counsellor must make the patient feel that he is a worth-while person and that the long hours spent on successive interviews are by no means wasted. The communication of this knowledge is the *sine qua non* of recovery.

There is no doubt that Freud, with his method of free association, the encouraging of patients to articulate their innermost thoughts without inhibition, stands behind this theory of acceptance. Nowadays this method is used by counsellors whatever school of psychological thought they may claim to belong to. Generally speaking, the attitude of acceptance is regarded as the opposite of the judgmental and moralistic approach. It is deliberately used to enable a person in bondage to some inhibiting fear, to articulate freely feelings which hitherto he has repressed. Non-authoritarian in character, the technique is used to create a sympathetic rapport between the counsellor who accepts and the patient who is accepted.

But acceptance is not a feather bed into which the patient sinks and forgets all his problems. On the contrary, it is an active function on the part of the counsellor who is prepared to adopt a positive understanding attitude towards the patient. Acceptance is not an expression of one individual opinion, but a consistent attitude of good will towards the patient no matter how nauseating his behaviour. The staff of an institution for emotionally disturbed adolescents may deliberately allow them to express their hatreds and feelings of inadequacy within a framework of acceptance. Only then will they begin to learn some inner controls. This strategy of 'turning the other cheek' is not a weak submissive gesture but a consciously thought-out, useful therapeutic tool.

Then again there is the technique of non-directive

counselling. This celebrated phrase was coined by Carl F. Rogers who is inclined to use counselling and psychotherapy as interchangeable terms. The counsellor must never offer a ready-made prescription to a patient who comes to him desperately looking for help. The sort of advice that is too specific is blind to the hidden stresses and conflicts of personality. It offers a premature, prefabricated solution which too often is discredited by the complexities of a developing human situation. According to Rogers, the counsellor ought to hand over the control of the interview to the patient. He asks few direct questions and his whole aim is to leave the patient to express himself as freely as possible in an open permissive atmosphere. In this way the patient is encouraged to gain a deeper insight into his own predicament and in the process to grow in understanding and maturity. The question we must ask ourselves, however, is whether non-directive counselling is in fact possible and if possible desirable.

Whatever the apostles of non-directiveness say, it is certain that the physical presence of a counsellor in the same room as the patient exerts some kind of directive influence. He may try to be scrupulously neutral but his occasional grunts, his monosyllabic interjections, his facial grimaces, the look in his eye, can be powerfully reinforcing. In addition to the personality of the counsellor himself there are other factors—the pictures hanging on the wall, the various pieces of furniture, the status symbols however unobtrusive—reminding the patient that the man sitting across the desk from him is a member of a respected profession. All these facts in combination with the I–Thou interaction of two personalities militate against the ideal of non-directiveness.

In social case-work there has been a gradual departure from the non-directive method of counselling brought about by various pragmatic considerations. In current thinking the need for ego-therapy is heavily stressed. What is more, it is now conceded that improvement can sometimes take place without insight, and that there are certain situations where insight may exacerbate the patient's condition. Social workers will no doubt try their best to dispel ignorance, but any attempt at ego reinforcement demands some form of selection. Some defences of the personality will be singled out and an effort will be made to strengthen them. Others will be ignored or actively discouraged. And this is not possible without conscious directiveness on the part of the social worker. The truth is that the counsellor who is anxious to become an instrument of healing must accept the paradox of non-involved involvement and non-judgmental directiveness.

The Rogerian emphasis on non-directiveness became pervasive in the USA over the last few decades. It influenced men like Seward Hiltner and Paul Johnston who, though they disagreed with the master on minor details, became its passionate advocates. But of late a strong reaction against this method of counselling has set in all over the world. In his book *The Faith of the Counsellors* Paul Halmos refers to non-directive counselling as a fiction and goes out of his way to discredit it. In the USA H. J. Clinebell proposes 'a multiple methodology' instead of the Rogers' client-centred non-directive methodology. While retaining an attitude of respect to the patient the counsellor will select different methods of dealing with a counselling situation, each method being appropriate to the person and the problem. This approach has sometimes been described as the 'eclectic method'. Each individual ought to assume responsibility for his own life, but in actual life many people are unable to solve their problems and so they need the sympathy and support of a counsellor. In such a situation, the counsellor, while remaining as open-minded and non-authoritarian as possible, is forced to take the initiative and offer some measure of directiveness.

(3) *Pastoral Counselling*
In his book *Counselling in the United States* Harrop Freeman, Professor of Law at Cornell University, examines the various methods of counselling used by the older professions: Law,

Medicine and the Clergy. He accuses lawyers of being too directive, over confident of their own prescriptions and not at all inclined to refer. Of doctors, where counselling is concerned, he takes an even dimmer view. Too many of them, he says, are suspicious of psychotherapy while lacking the basic rudiments of counselling. What outrages Freeman is that while medical schools can on the whole command brighter candidates than either Law or Church, the end product seems to be cast in a mould. He regards ministers as better trained and more flexible in dealing with people and their problems. He attributes this to the kind of education they receive and to the training they get in psychotherapy in the various theological colleges. Professor Freeman may very well be right, but such a summing up should not tempt ministers in the direction of smugness and complacency. As a profession they can still be too authoritarian and in interviews they are apt to dominate and talk too much.

Pastoral counselling has a distinctive role but it cannot be separated altogether from other forms of counselling, all of which are based on an understanding of personal relationship. The minister of religion and the avowedly agnostic counsellor practise the technique we call acceptance and this acceptance extends to the whole man. It embraces everything: his intellectual capacity, his natural talents, his emotional tensions and traumas. The counsellor accepts the social failures every bit as much as the man who has reached the pinnacles of success. Even when the patient is guilty of violations of the civil and moral law, he is guaranteed acceptance by the counsellor.

Professor Tillich argues that the principle of acceptance shared by agnostic and Christian psychotherapists is a bridge which spans the different disciplines of psychology and theology. He goes further and argues that this well-known method of counselling demonstrates the meaning of the reformed doctrine of Justification by Faith. In his *The Shaking of the Foundations* he writes, 'It happens; or it does not happen. And certainly it does not happen if we try to force it upon ourselves, just as it shall not happen so long as we think, in our self-complacency, that we have no need of it. Grace strikes us when we are in great pain and restlessness. It strikes us when we walk through the dark valley of a meaningless and empty life. It strikes us when we feel that our separation is deeper than usual, because we have violated another life, a life which we loved, or from which we were estranged. It strikes us when our disgust for our own being, our indifference, our weakness, our hostility, and our lack of direction and composure have become intolerable to us. It strikes us when, year after year, the longed-for perfection of life does not appear, when the old compulsions reign within us as they have for decades, when despair destroys all joy and courage. Sometimes at that moment a wave of light breaks into our darkness, and it is as though a voice were saying: "You are accepted. You are accepted, accepted by that which is greater than you, and the name of which you do not know. Do not ask for the name now; perhaps you will find it later. Do not try to do anything now; perhaps later you will do much. Do not seek for anything; do not perform anything; do not intend anything. Simply accept the fact that you are accepted".'

Nevertheless, pastoral counselling does differ from other forms of counselling in that its purpose is not only to help a person to improve his relationship with others, and to clarify his self understanding, but also to say something helpful about the human-divine relationship. God cannot be left out of pastoral counselling. Furthermore, if the parishioner has deliberately singled out a minister, ethical and religious questions are bound to arise. This may not alter the principles and techniques used in the interview, but it is likely to affect the direction which the counselling takes.

The problem for the minister counsellor is how to resolve the ambiguity between acceptance and approval. If he is to be effective, the counsellor must never show moral disapproval or shock when someone confesses. To do this is to alienate the patient from the very start. The uncongenial qualities of the patient—his truculence, paranoic rages and compulsions—must be revealed in an accepting atmosphere, otherwise he will not co-operate. But this does not mean that the counsellor necessarily approves of them. The Christian counsellor has his own belief, and his convictions about what constitutes right and wrong in human behaviour. If these convictions are introduced at the wrong moment, they are likely to be interpreted as censorious and judg-mental, and the whole counselling process is ruined. The counsellor must first of all accept the ethical situation and then choose the appropriate moment when he discloses his own moral convictions. The timing is all-important. Donald Evans, writing on 'Pastoral Counselling and Traditional Theology' in the *Scottish Journal of Theology* observes: 'Where a person is in a situation of psychological threat and accepts only these interpretations which enable him to evade his real problem, it is usually useless and sometimes dangerous to present Christian doctrines. Non-directive therapy may help him to gain self knowledge which leads to mental health and maturity; pastors may use it as part of their healing in such cases. When this stage is reached, there is a place for rational discussion or persuasion regarding doctrine.'

In pastoral counselling the positive resources of the Christian faith must not be forgotten. In an age of unbelief and uncertainty it offers an ultimate purpose and an ultimate hope. In an age of anxiety it offers comfort, not the chloroform-mask variety, but the kind that fortifies a man so that he can face up to challenge, even calamity with a large measure of equanimity. And none of us can under-estimate the inspiration and motivating power a man can draw from worship, preaching, the fellowship of the Church and the celebration of the sacraments. Faith in a caring God, demonstrated in the world by ministers who are concerned with people, and by a community of authentic believers, may be just the right milieu for those who are frightened and are sick because they have always run away from close human relationship.

The good minister of the future will be a man who will have a better understanding of the relation between theology and psychology. He will also be a skilled counsellor; who will use his psychological insight along with available religious resources to help his parishioners meet and triumph over the troubles that assail them. There are philosophical and practical differences of great magnitude between theology and psychology but they share a common interest in man, his quirks, his predicaments, his potentialities and his needs. They also have a common aim—the giving of solace and reassurance and the mediation of healing. The enlightened minister is one who is an agent of healing, not only in the special area of pastoral counselling, but in the whole of pastoral care, from sermon to sacrament, pageantry to prayer, belief to benediction.

12. THE MINISTRY OF REFERRAL

Every minister, however well qualified he may be in theology and skilled in psychology, is bound sooner or later to meet pastoral problems which are beyond his resources. If he happens to be authoritarian by nature he may be tempted to rely on a set strategy for every eventuality that arises. In every situation, however subtle or complex, he is inclined to convey a bland assurance of undisputed mastery. He will attempt everything without due regard to the severe limitations imposed on him by life itself. This kind of minister is a positive menace. In the end of the day he invariably turns out to be a dismal failure.

At the other end of the referral spectrum we find the minister who has no confidence in himself. He automatically refers every problem to someone else. Assuming that the secular psychotherapist is better qualified to understand and unravel the emotional disturbances of his parishioners, he makes no effort to engage with them on a deep pastoral level. In doing this he turns his back on the healing resources which from the very beginning have characterised the Christian faith.

The good minister is one who avoids these twin errors. Aware of the authoritarian bias of his own nature, he deliberately curbs it in order to be more open to others. Overwhelmed as he often is by the obdurate complexity of so many pastoral problems, he refuses to take refuge in a fatalistic cynicism. Conscious of his own inadequacy, nevertheless he is ready to adopt a positive attitude to the opportunities put in his way. At the same time he is prepared to accept help from whatever source. Spurning the paranoic loneliness of those who feel sorry for themselves, he joins the company of those who 'bear one another's burdens and so fulfil the law of Christ'.

If, with Paul, Augustine, Luther and Professor Reinold Niebuhr, we accept guilt not as fantasy but fact, a minister is wrong in referring every case to the secular psychiatrist and psychoanalyst. He should be able to help the parishioner towards a deeper understanding and a more resolute acceptance of the meaning of forgiveness. But while this is so, in his appraisal of the situation the minister may become aware of a degree of disorder that indicates the need for referral. The wider his experience, the more sensitive he becomes to danger signals, pointing in the direction of depth-therapy. These signals include depression, extreme emotionalism, dreamy detachment, withdrawal from social contact, delusional grandeur, paronoic blaming of other people, the objectivising of experience as if what happened to the patient was actually happening to someone else. What I wish to say about the ministry of referral I include under three separate heads.

(1) *The When of Referral*

Shakespeare talks of the 'tide in the affairs of men', the opportune hour that calls out for action. Tillich speaks of 'kairos', which means not chronological time, but the moment of truth when the converging forces coalesce and cry out for creative action. It is the same with a minister in the process of pastoral counselling. He never refers a parishioner mechanically, not even those who are in need of immediate attention. He waits for the 'kairos', the creative moment, the right time to act. This demands a combination of Christian humility and professional skill.

As I have said already, there are ministers who are over-eager to refer. Afraid that something will go wrong with a parishioner he has counselled, he is inclined to panic. What happens if the couple he has interviewed in the end decide on divorce? In the eyes of the congregation the minister's image will be affected. What happens if the depressed person he is trying to help commits suicide? What would the congregation think if they knew that the member he sees so often is a practising homosexual? While we cannot disregard such fears we must remember that the Christian gospel does not protect any man from the risk of misunderstanding. If it is true that the human malaise in all its baffling expressions stems from estrangement from God, there can be no healing till the broken disrupted relationship is restored. While a minister must be grateful to the expert, he must never belittle the resources of a faith that can remove mountains.

On the other hand, some ministers are far too slow in referring their parishioners to the expert. The hesitation is due to various causes. The minister in question may feel that referral is a threat to his self esteem as a pastor. He may resent the fact that those who do not confess his faith are capable of solving human problems. This attitude is as old as the New Testament itself. In his Gospel Luke records 'John answered, Master we saw a man, casting out demons in your name and we forbade him, because he does not follow us. But Jesus said unto him, Do not forbid him for he that is not against you is for you.'

Another reason is the minister's distrustful attitude towards secular psychotherapy. In his eyes, sending a parishioner to a psychiatrist is a downright betrayal of the Gospel. The person sent will have his religion psychoanalysed out of him. Was not Freud an out-and-out atheist who hated the Church and described religion as 'a universal obsessional neurosis'? Are not so many psychotherapists irreligious and anti-clerical? No doubt this may be true, but the same minister will not object to an atheistic surgeon removing his septic tonsils.

In the difficult question of whom to refer, the condition of the parishioner is of primary importance. If his disorder is really serious, immediate referral seems to be the wisest course to pursue. But while this is undoubtedly true the condition of the minister is also a relevant consideration.

Even more so than in other professions, ministers vary enormously in knowledge, skill, emotional stability and in ability to handle others. In determining the 'when' of referral the following considerations must be kept in mind.

There is the problem of time. The ministry is a full-time man-sized occupation. Sermon preparation, the writing of prayers, visiting, administration, pastoral counselling and study are, between them, time-devouring. Whatever formula the minister has, there never is enough time. An alcoholic, a manic depressive contemplating suicide, an obsessional neurotic call for care and constant attention. Even if the problem is well within his professional know-how, he simply does not have the time.

There is also the question of skill. Though it is true that ministers today are much better trained in psychotherapy than they used to be, their expertise is still strictly limited. There are problems of pathological dimensions which demand treatment in depth. In Glasgow University all divinity students get a twenty-hour course in the Department of Psychological Medicine. They see all kinds of patients being interviewed: alcoholics, manic depressives, schizophrenics, neurotics and psychotics. Afterwards they are skilfully cross-examined by the consultant psychiatrist as to tell-tale symptoms. The tutor's advice to the class is starkly unambiguous. If the problem is a pathological one, refer. If not, use your own pastoral skill in conjunction with the healing resources of the congregation.

How many interviews should take place before the parishioner is referred? There is no simple answer to this question. But there is a rule of thumb that if the interviews reach five without any visible improvement, then the emotional disturbance is more severe than was at first supposed, and referral is indicated. Recently I interviewed a university student suffering from some form of obsessional neurosis. At the third interview I became convinced the treatment lay beyond my skill and resources and after some opposition I managed to arrange a meeting with a psychiatrist.

(2) *The How of Referral*

It goes without saying that the when, the how and the where
of referral can't be neatly separated. From beginning to end
they are inextricably mixed. Nevertheless, there is a sense
in which we can meaningfully talk of the 'how' of referral.
The parishioner has come for help. After two or three interviews the minister believes that referral is necessary. But how
to effect this delicate transaction without disrupting and
doing violence to the relationship which has been formed?
There are a number of hurdles, by no means imaginary
ones, which have to be cleared before any progress is made.

One of the hurdles is paradoxically enough the access-
ibility of the minister. He can foster a feeling of negative
dependence in the parishioner. Not that a sense of dependence
in itself is a bad thing. To a certain extent all of us, however
mature, are dependent on other people. But when dependence
on the minister becomes a crutch, the parishioner becomes
increasingly unwilling to assume the responsibility which
normally is the badge of maturity. If this happens each
succeeding interview has the effect of postponing the healing
process, and the minister is faced with the unenviable task
of terminating the meetings.

The relationship which develops between minister and
parishioner can be so complex and subtle that it defies any
attempt at a straightforward analysis. The parishioner
sometimes manipulates the minister. He uses him as a sort
of emotional aspirin that temporarily eases his distress, a
soothing anodyne, a pastoral codeine tablet which treats
the surface symptoms but ignores the radical disease. It
sometimes happens that the minister enjoys this kind of
interview every bit as much as the parishioner. It makes him
feel good for it panders to his sense of self importance. Perhaps
all ministers have a 'saviour syndrome'. They resent the
spurning of their help and the seeking of it somewhere else.

Another hurdle that has to be surmounted is open resistance to referral on part of the parishioner. The reasons
for the point blank refusal vary a great deal and can be
exceedingly complex. The parishioner may be afraid of

psychologists, regarding them as professional brain-washers, practitioners of a dark and nefarious cult. Or he may be afraid only of deep excavation. Like the priest in *The Diary of a Country Priest*, suspecting that there is something radically wrong, he prefers the discomfort to the discovery of the truth.

There are instances where referral presents no problems. The parishioner gladly accepts the direction proferred. This is especially true of alcoholics who have touched rock bottom. But how does the minister proceed when the parishioner rationalises, procrastinates and generally proves as slippery as an eel? Are there any guiding principles which can help him in difficult situations? There are in fact a number of useful insights which have emerged out of the cumulative experience of Christian counselling over the last few decades.

(*a*) The minister's basic concern should be not for his own professional reputation but for the health of his parishioner. This sounds ridiculously elementary but too often it is a principle which is lost sight of.

(*b*) The referral must not be effected in such a way as to imply rejection by the minister. After all, the parishioner has singled out the minister for help, and he resents being bundled off to a so-called expert who is a total stranger.

(*c*) The referral must take place with the co-operation of the parishioner. He cannot be forced to go to a psychiatrist against his will. It may be difficult to persuade the patient, but unless he participates in the decision there is no healing.

(*d*) The minister must not contract out the moment he hands the parishioner over to a psychiatrist. He must continue to visit and support him through the entire ordeal.

The 'how' of referral is not a mechanical operation. It demands first and foremost a passionate concern for the well-being of the parishioner. In addition it calls for tact, insight and a large measure of persuasiveness. The minister may be an amateur in the world of psychotherapy, but he is indispensable in the delicate transaction we call referral. If he is the one who enables a disturbed parishioner to establish a healthy relationship with a recognised expert, then indeed he has performed a great service.

(3) *The Where of Referral*

The moment a minister goes to a congregation, he ought to familiarise himself with all the sources of help available to him in the city or region in which he works. This is important, for sometimes all that is necessary for referral is the possession of the appropriate information. Efficiency in this respect is good for his image in the community. Once he gets a name for it, all kinds of pastoral opportunities are opened up. While the sources of help available to the minister are in a sense limitless, there are certain people to whom he instinctively turns.

(a) *The Doctor*

Traditionally there has been a substantial measure of mutual respect and co-operation between the clerical and medical professions. But ironically enough, since the advent of counselling, tensions have built up on both sides. The average doctor is apt to regard a minister who dabbles in psychotherapy as a dangerous quack. On the other hand, the psychologically minded minister tends to regard the orthodox General Practitioner as a dedicated Hippocratic reactionary.

It is encouraging to see that of late a bridge is being built across the chasm of mutual suspicions and antagonisms. I have spoken to a number of Pastoral Association groups throughout the country in which doctors have been rather prominent. The American Medical Association, by no means the most radical of institutions, has established a Department of Religion and Medicine. Under the National Health Service in Great Britain, a minister who refers a parishioner to a psychiatrist must do so through the local General Practitioner.

(b) The Psychiatrist

Here again mutual antagonism may exist. Some psychiatrists feel that ministers exacerbate the sense of guilt which they, the psychiatrists, are trying to remove in non-religious ways. There are ministers on the other hand who regard secular psychiatrists as saboteurs of the faith. They do not recognise the reality of sin, and the therapeutic transaction is a cheap and dubious business.

> 'I've been on one of those "complex" tours
> I want you to make my problem yours
> Now gimmie one of them cut rate cures
> Shrinker man.'

No doubt there are faults on both sides. Distrust cannot be removed overnight. But co-operation between the two professions is imperative. A minister who, in the course of an interview with a parishioner, sees clear signs of pathological disorder is duty bound to refer him to a reputable psychiatrist.

(c) The Psychologist

Here I am thinking of a man who has no medical degree, but has acquired clinical qualifications and can put up his plate as a psychoanalyst. Their attitudes to religion vary widely. I know one psychoanalyst who would unhesitatingly call himself an agnostic, yet could be described as a sort of secular saint, like Dr Rieux in Camus' novel *The Plague*. His compassion for people in trouble seems inexhaustible. I know another who is a devout Catholic. He believes in harnessing the spiritual resources of Church and community to help his patients. On a number of occasions I have referred parishioners to psychologists, Christian and agnostic, and I have not been disappointed.

(d) The Social Service Agencies

In Britain these services are well developed and, thanks to the National Health Service, available to all in need 'without money and without price'. They cover a wide range of problems—juvenile delinquency, adoption, marriage breakdown, abandoned children, the mentally handicapped, and that of old people. Ministers should approach such agencies without pre-arranged dogmatic solutions to exceedingly complex problems. Intelligent and sensitive co-operation is called for between the two professions.

(e) The Clergy

From the very beginning in the history of the Christian Church, certain ministers have demonstrated unique gifts in the 'cure of souls'. It is only recently that standards have been set up for ministers who feel a call to this kind of vocation. Developments in the USA have proceeded further than in Great Britain. Professor Hobart Mowrer, the psychologist, advocates a counselling 'group practice' among ministers, under expert supervision. The Kokomo experiment in Indiana is a model of this kind of development. Mowrer is also in favour of certain ministers specialising in psychotherapy, who could accept referrals from their ministers and psychologists on a fee basis.

Divinity students as well as ministers frequently complain that they lack the authority possessed by a doctor or a Catholic priest. Professor Mowrer may be right in accusing Protestant ministers of referring too many cases to secular psychotherapists. Beyond any question the minister has resources at his command which he is loth to use. I discovered this in prison camp where neither doctor nor psychiatrist was always available. The minister is first and foremost a theologian, so he is not unduly impressed by the glib pronouncements of psychoanalysts who equate sin with superstition. On the other hand, because he is a pastor, he must remain sensitive to the most recent developments in psychotherapy. In the measure in which a minister submits himself to the twin disciplines of theology and psychotherapy, he will recover the authority which used to be his, the departure of which he so understandably regrets.

BIOGRAPHICAL AND BIBLIOGRAPHICAL NOTES
TO PART FOUR: THE MINISTER AS PASTOR

10. IMPORTANCE OF PSYCHOTHERAPY

B. F. Skinner
Professor of Psychology at Harvard University. A dedicated behaviourist, he argues that we cannot afford freedom. His experiments have been done mainly with pigeons and rats. Some years ago there was a delightful cartoon in an American magazine, poking fun at Skinner. It shows two rats inside a contraption. Looking formidably intelligent, one rat says to the other 'Boy, have I got this guy conditioned! Every time I press the bar down, he drops in a piece of food'. His best-known works are *The Behaviour Organisms* and *Walden Two*.

Joseph Wolpe
A South African psychiatrist, now at Templeton University, USA. A behaviourist, he claims that what we call a neurosis is not evidence of unconscious conflict, but a bad habit which can be corrected by the appropriate conditioning.

R. D. Laing
A psychiatrist who has worked with the Tavistock Institute and is now Director of the Langham Clinic, London. He has studied different modes of consciousness, especially those induced by drugs. He has a particular interest in schizophrenia. His best-known works are *The Politics of Experience and the Sweet Bird of Paradise* and *The Divided Self*.

Franz Kafka
The creative novelist who has profoundly influenced modern literature. In his novels he presents man seeking to justify his existence in an absurd world. He deplores the tortuous ramifications of bureaucracy and the stranglehold of systems. His best-known works are *The Trial* and *The Castle*.

11. THE ROLE OF THE COUNSELLOR

Sigmund Freud The Viennese doctor and psychologist who was the real founder of psychoanalysis. He attached enormous importance to the unconscious and to infancy. He regarded religion as some sort of universal neurosis. Post-Freudians like Jung, Adler and Horney accused him of over-emphasising the biological at the expense of social and cultural conditioning. Among his best-known works are *Beyond the Pleasure Principle*, *Fundamentals of Psycho Analysis* and *Totem and Taboo*.

Carl F. Rogers

His name is associated with 'non-directive counselling'. To him the end of counselling is what he calls 'the process'. One of his best-known works is *On Becoming a Person*. He has exercised a powerful, far-reaching influence on psychotherapy.

12. THE MINISTRY OF REFERRAL

Albert Camus

The existentialist novelist who stressed the absurdity of human existence and, at the same time, the need for social justice and individual compassion. His best-known works are *The Outsider*, *The Plague* and *The Fall*.

Hobart Mowrer

Professor of Psychology at the University of Indiana. Sceptical of the worth of psychoanalysis, he predicts its demise within a generation or so. His attack on the doctrine of Justification by Faith is based on a misunderstanding of both Paul and Luther. He argues in favour of a Protestant system of penance. His best-known work is *The Crisis in Psychiatry and Religion*.

Part Five

THE MINISTER AS PROPHET

13. INVOLVEMENT IN POLITICS

Politics is the art of the possible. So said Aristotle long ago. In that celebrated statement the Greek philosopher implied that life is a maddeningly complex business, that in the realm of human relationship there are no straightforward answers, no simplistic solutions, and that we are wasting our time in looking for them. The pure ideal may exist somewhere, but in a world riven by competing interests and colliding loyalties, it cannot be implemented. All we can hope for is some sort of workable compromise, what Professor Niebuhr liked to call 'the proximate good'.

Among Christians and indeed among many humanists there is a deep-seated prejudice against any mixing of religion with politics. One reason for this attitude is a historical one. In the past the Church did get mixed up in politics in a most unsalutary manner. The historian Professor Butterfield claims that when the Church occupied the seat of power, she was every bit as ruthless as communism in her attitude to non-conformists. The plight of Ulster rather poignantly illustrates that a marriage between religion and politics can be a far from happy one. I wonder if Randolph Churchill (Winston's father) foresaw the consequences of the policy he spelt out for the Unionists in North Ireland when he directed them to go in on the orange ticket.

Another reason for the widespread antagonism to mixing religion and politics, one might call theological. It is the tacit unexamined assumption that the proper sphere of religion is man's soul and the world beyond, while the proper sphere of politics is the physical needs of men and women, in short the world here and now. This dichotomy between the spiritual and the secular, between the spirit and the body has

139

a long history, stretching as far back as the Manichean heresy, to which the great Augustine for a time succumbed. The complete separation of politics and religion is insisted upon in all totalitarian states. In Russia the practice of religion is permitted, provided it keeps its nose clean and does not interfere in the affairs of the state. The same was true in Nazi Germany. Hitler and his cohorts encouraged a national religion to act as a buttress to their own demonic ideology. It was when men like Niemoller, Schneider and Bonhoeffer rallied the Christian ranks, declaring that Christianity was implacably opposed to the Nazi ideology, that the Church got into trouble. In South Africa, prime minister Vorster is a passionate devotee of religion as long as it concentrates on prayer, preaching, comforting the afflicted and burying the dead. The moment it exceeds these bounds, it becomes an enemy of the state. The white rulers of Rhodesia more or less adopt the same attitude.

The Biblical faith is very different. The Old Testament prophets regarded religion as an intensely personal affair. Jehovah called certain men by name. He singled them out and issued a peremptory summons they could not refuse. The divine call was never doubted. It was not interpreted as an irrational compulsion explicable in terms of the Freudian super ego. It was the living God himself who called them. It was he who made them leave the vine they were dressing and the herd they were tending and sent them out to witness amid the maelstrom of Middle East politics.

But despite the intensely personal nature of their faith the prophets never once succumbed to pietism. Unlike Stalin, Hitler, Vorster, Ian Smith and the bulk of ordinary Christians, they were not guilty of the privatization of religion. The great prophets were called not to attain individual salvation, but to proclaim the will of God to the princes and politicians of their time. To an Isaiah, a Jeremiah or an Amos individual pietism was utterly unintelligible. The God they proclaimed was the Sovereign Lord of history, the one whose mighty hand rested firmly on the helm of things. The distinction which we draw between individual and historical faith was inconceivable to them. To separate these two dimensions of faith would be as destructive as separating the white and red corpuscles of the blood would be to life itself. To them the meaning of faith was commitment to God within the context of secular history.

When we come to the New Testament the position is a little more ambiguous. In the first century the relation of Christians to the state was very different from the twentieth-century position. At that time Palestine was an occupied nation, a helpless satellite of Roman imperial power. Christians had no vote and therefore no political responsibility. So in the New Testament we get no precise, specific, political guidance, useful for contemporary Christians, who by virtue of possessing a vote share in the authority of the state. But while this is so the New Testament does draw attention to two distinct attitudes which between them throw a certain amount of light on the complex relation that has always existed between Church and state.

The first attitude finds expression in Paul's Epistle to the Romans 13 and in 1 Peter 2. Paul enjoins Christians to be subject to the higher powers: 'The powers that be are ordained of God'. The passage in 1 Peter is largely a paraphrase of Romans 13: 'Be subject for the Lord's sake to every human institution, whether it be the emperor as supreme, or the governors as sent by him to punish those who do wrong and to praise those who do right'. Down the centuries these two passages have become the classic proof texts of political despotism. Rulers have used these two injunctions time and again to buttress every conceivable form of political injustice.

Paul and the author of 1 Peter show a remarkably optimistic attitude towards the state. According to the two passages referred to, the state is a God-given institution, necessary for the maintenance of law and order in society. For this reason Christians are under an obligation to obey its every injunction. This positive attitude to the state may be partly explained by the particular context out of which it springs. But behind the cultural conditioning there lurks a permanently valid insight. It is the recognition that government is a providential order, that without some sort of government, even bad government, society would disintegrate into a state of anarchy.

The New Testament, however, provides us with one other attitude to the state which can on no account be described as positive or optimistic. It is unambiguously expressed in the Book of Revelation. This strange book was written at a time when the conflict between Church and State had come to a head-on collision. The State which Paul calls 'God's servant for your good' is described by the author of Revelation as 'a blasphemous beast, making war upon the saints'. The writer does not advocate organised political resistance, but he does enjoin passive resistance, even to the point of suffering and death. We can count it fortunate that this enigmatic book was included in the canon, otherwise we would have no record of the church's resistance to a despotic state with demonic pretentions. In the Book of Revelation we look in vain for explicit political guidance, but it makes it clear that there are times when Christians must obey God rather than men.

There is no straight line between the radical ethic of the New Testament and the political ambiguities and relativities of the twentieth century, and it is foolish to look for a blueprint which is applicable to the contemporary situation. There is no specific programme, no simple panacea. But while the New Testament offers no clear-cut formula for our political predicaments, it does provide us with a number of insights. There are at least three.

(a) There must be political authority. Without it society will soon degenerate into a state of savage anarchy. It is the sort of insight which William Golding develops in his symbolical novel *Lord of the Flies*.

(b) For this very reason Christians ought to adopt a positive attitude towards the state. If people are to live together in peace, they need sanctions. Grace can only operate within a framework of laws.

(c) At the same time vigilance is imperative. We are all indebted to the state for many privileges and benefits but we must watch that the state does not exceed its proper bounds. Democratic structures and processes demand eternal vigilance.

In the area of political conflict which exists in many parts of the world, in South Africa, in Rhodesia, in North Ireland, and which simmers under the surface in all societies, are there any strategies which Christians can implement? Must they resign themselves to a dual standard for personal and public life? There is one kind of Christian morality which obtains in personal relationships, another which applies to society and the world of nations. This attitude is more characteristic perhaps of Lutheranism than it is of either Catholicism or Calvinism. Its weakness consists in its failure to subject social issues to some sort of Christian critique. To apply the ethic of Jesus to political life is exceedingly difficult, but to withhold Christian criticism in the area of political conflict is to open the door to a cynical and ruthless despotism. Let us then consider a number of possible strategies which in varying degrees may be relevant to the problem of social and political conflict.

(1) *The strategy of the identification of Christianity with a particular political or social structure*

For Christians down the centuries, this has been a recurring temptation. This was the hidden, unspoken assumption behind the phenomenon of McCarthyism in America, the implicit belief that democracy represented the dimension of absolute good, and communism that of absolute evil. Karl Barth, the foremost theologian of our age, took up a very different attitude. He adopted a lofty neutrality during the Cold War, even at the time of the Hungarian rising. Claiming that the judgment of God rested upon both East and West, he refused to take sides.

The ambiguities and relativities of political life rule out 'Christian politics'. There are technical issues affecting political judgments on which Christians are bound to disagree. In addition there are preferences based on differing emphases. Conflicting interpretations may exist on questions of law and order, on the meaning of freedom, on indignation over existing injustices. It makes a considerable difference, how near or menacing the particular evils are to one's own experience. Because of this and other reasons, it is pointless to look for unanimity among Christians on political questions.

In some countries there are Christian political parties sometimes Protestant, sometimes Catholic and sometimes mixed. The Christian Democrats in West Germany, though predominantly Roman Catholic, present a good example of a mixed party. In Holland, Protestant parties tend to have a strong Calvinistic ethos. It is significant that after the war a large section of the leadership broke away from the two Protestant parties and joined secular Socialists to form a Labour Party. These Christians felt that vis-à-vis the contemporary crises, religious political parties had lost the reason for their existence, and that in order to fulfil their vocation, they had to join forces with their secular brethren.

Christian political parties manage to misrepresent the true situation. They give the impression that Christianity implies a particular political programme, whereas this is not so. In the process they succeed in draining off from secular parties a Christian influence which could be healthy. They also have a knack of bestowing a false sanctity on the inevitable compromises of politics. Worst of all they are prone to bring with them the fanaticism and self-righteousness which belong to a certain kind of religion. Instead of helping to integrate, they are more likely to precipitate a deep spiritual chasm in the life of a nation. All political structures, including programmes congenial to Christian ethics, lie under the Divine Judgment. The weakness of the strategy we have outlined is that of introducing religious absolutes into the comparative judgments of history.

(2) *The Strategy of Pacifism*

It is perhaps useful to distinguish between two kinds of pacifism. There is the absolute pacifist who refuses to countenance war in any circumstance. If he is a Christian he holds that war in all its aspects is a categorical denial of all that we mean by Christian love. If he is a humanist he rejects war on the ground that it is destructive of our highest values and tragically abortive in that it succeeds only in exacerbating the dilemmas it sets out to solve. The absolute pacifist stance may range from the extreme position taken up by Tolstoy, to those adopted by contemporary Christians like Professor Roland Bainton of America, Lord Soper and Lord MacLeod in Britain. It is hardly necessary to mention the courage of those protagonists of a pacifist strategy. They do not counsel monastic withdrawal but insist on political involvement and costly commitment.

There is also the pragmatic pacifist, who is suspicious of military establishments and deplores war even as a last resort. There are wars like Vietnam and others on which he is prepared to adopt an undeviating pacifist position. But he is not absolutist in that in certain circumstances, such as the Second World War, he feels compelled to bear arms. Bertrand Russell illustrates the point perfectly. In the First World War, he was an uncompromising pacifist. As a result he lost his professorship and went to prison. After Hitler's rise to power Russell underwent a radical change of heart. As concentration camps began to sprout all over Germany and Jews were driven like animals into gas ovens, Russell vociferously clamoured for war. Nazism was so evil that co-existence with it was not possible. Its defeat demanded the kind of surgery which refuses to stop short of war.

The dilemma of pacifism is focussed most sharply for us in the realm of foreign policy. The absolute pacifist would have us renounce nuclear weapons, unilaterally, whatever the intentions of Russia may be. If this policy were accepted, it would follow that the free world would be subject to Communist pressure of a blackmailing kind. There would be no need for overt aggression. The non-pacifist argument is that by refusing to abandon the ultimate deterrent, this can be prevented from happening, without provoking an atomic war. What the absolute pacifist fails to see is that while the local community can be built by many forms of mutual trust, the world community cannot be built, initially, on mutual trust. To preach mutual trust is pointless in a situation where historic facts create mutual fear. But there is a possibility that a stabilised situation of mutual fear, in which resistance to a political dogma prevents the premature victory of that dogma, may finally create a community of common responsibility towards the future of mankind.

(3) *The Strategy of Direct Action*

This can be defined as attempts to change or modify the existing social structures. It may in some situations consist of no more than exerting pressure and using propaganda within the framework of existing democratic institutions. But the democratic processes can be used by rulers not only to accelerate but also to impede and prevent progress. When this happens Christians may resolve to step outside the framework of normal democratic structures into open resistance to policies which are deemed to be fundamentally unjust. Within recent years this has happened all over the world. The Civil Rights movement in the United States gained momentum and in a short time proved irresistible when 'sit-ins' were staged in defiance of the law all over the South.

There are other situations so unjust and so impervious to persuasive, non-coercive tactics that Christians, however much they hate it, have to resort to violence. This is what happened to Oliver Cromwell in his fight against the absolutism of the Stuarts. When he had exhausted all the democratic processes he was forced to take up the sword. A more recent example was the abortive plot against the Nazi regime in 1944. Among those who organised it were men of Christian conscience with a concern not only for their own country but also for the future of Western civilisation. They were motivated by the conviction that in this tragic situation nothing short of violence would meet the demands of Christian responsibility for the neighbour.

Challenging for the mass of conformist Christians is the fact that Dietrich Bonhoeffer, the martyr theologian, sponsored the sort of direct action which involved violence. This was also true of many other Christians in Nazi-occupied countries. In participating in the Resistance Movement they were by no means blind to the logic of their commitment. It meant aiding and abetting violence in many forms, including that of assassination. Count Staufenberg was a devout practising Catholic. In carrying the attache case containing the bomb meant to kill Hitler and by placing it against the leg of the table at which the Führer was sitting, he was deliberately and cold-bloodedly implementing a policy of violence, albeit in the interests of justice. Christian action can be thought of as a spectrum bounded at one end by democratic activity, and at the other by revolution, with non-violent activity somewhere in between.

(4) *The Strategy of Indirect Action*

In his book *Christians and the State*, Professor John C. Bennett argues convincingly that the strategy of indirect action on the part of Christians is in the long run far more important than that of direct action. He claims that the Church has at least three kinds of indirect influence.

(*a*) There is the Church's long-term influence on and shaping of the ethos, the values, and the moral sensibilities of society. History offers an abundance of examples. One is that of the Catholic Church in a Europe emerging from the Dark Ages. Another is the influence of Puritanism on the public life of Britain in the seventeenth century. A century later there were the social and political repercussions of the Wesley revival. It is impossible to assess the influence of a dynamic faith in nurturing the conscience of a community.

(*b*) There is the accidental by-product result of a Church

seeking to be true to herself. In Nazi Germany the Church proved to be by far the toughest opposition to overcome. This was an important factor in reconciliation across national lines immediately after the war. And the stand taken by the Church in the USA gave a tremendous boost to the Civil Rights movement.

(c) Finally there is the indirect influence exerted by Christian teaching on some of the great issues of society. As John Knox said long ago, an informed mind is our best bulwark against tyranny and our shield against prejudice. There are a number of hopeful signs that such teaching is bearing fruit. Christians are becoming more sensitive to the scandal of race and more critical of economic injustice. This is certainly true of ministers and shows itself on congregation and theological college levels.

To what extent is the Christian faith applicable to politics in what remains of the twentieth century? It may fail to present us with what could be described as a practical policy, but it succeeds in sharpening our insights. It reminds of the fragmentariness and fragility of all human virtues. It also reminds us of the destructive as well as the creative possibilities of human freedom. It will not allow the pietists to forget that religion is rooted in social solidarity. It is never a private, esoteric, individualistic affair. The prophet is not an apostle of the occult nor a champion of spookiness. He is rather one who interprets with sensitivity what is happening in the present and intelligently interprets the pull of the future, one who recognises the moment of truth when it comes, what Tillich calls the genuine 'kairos'. Suspicious of all *status quo* ideologies, the prophet knows that God acts not only in individual lives, but also in social and political structures. Christian commitment is first and foremost commitment to Christ, but commitment to him ought to carry with it a commitment to clear political perception.

14. PLACE OF SOCIOLOGY

Sociology developed from the philosophical, moral and political concerns of the early nineteenth century. The name itself was coined by Auguste Comte, the French philosopher, who claimed that sociology had displaced theology as queen of the sciences. This belief, stripped of some of its more fantastic pretensions, crossed the Atlantic and began to exert a strong influence on American academic life. In the New World its enthusiastic protagonists regarded it as a science, every bit as accurate as mathematics and all-comprehensive in its scope. There was, I believe, a solemn memorandum presented to Brown University, suggesting that all other departments should be re-grouped under that of sociology. Needless to say this early arrogance is not so obtrusive now. There are, however, academics of the more traditional cast who still regard sociology as an obstreperous and outrageous upstart and who would dearly like to see it cut down to what they call its proper size.

Sociology has been defined as 'the study of systems of social actions and their inter-relations'. It deals with institutions, social organisations, patterns of culture, and for this reason there can be no clear-cut dichotomy between it and theology. While possessing a transcendent dimension, religion is rooted in society. It speaks to the individual in the deep and secret places that defy conceptual analysis, but it also expresses itself in solid, visible, identifiable institutions. There is no such thing as a faith which has come to men straight out of heaven. On the contrary it is born within a particular context of history, is moulded by a particular pattern of culture, and to a certain extent is shaped by the language in which it seeks to express its basic beliefs. From this it follows that theology and sociology must be in constant dialogue. Only thus will religion divest itself of the suffocating provincialisms and narrow dogmatisms that obscure its true nature. Theology needs the social sciences in order to examine its own culturally conditioned formulations, and at the same time to see more clearly what it should declare as of divine human import.

Sociology—Friend or Foe?
The same principle of ambivalence that pervades the whole of life applies in large measure to sociology. Science is the example par excellence of this. No one can exaggerate the benefits it has bestowed on mankind. It has raised life expectation, reduced infant mortality and, to a degree bordering on the miraculous, controlled diseases that once decimated the people of entire continents. At the same time it possesses powers of limitless destruction, in the shape of deadly germs, atomic bombs and inter-continental missiles. To a lesser degree this ambivalence is part and parcel of sociology.

Beyond any doubt sociologists by their investigations have influenced penological practice in the western world. It is questionable whether the abolition of capital punishment in Britain would have come so early as it did, if sociologists had not discredited mass prejudice with some solid statistics. The American Supreme Court's 1954 decision to desegregate schools was not taken all of a sudden. It was based on a number of sociological surveys, on the effect of segregation in schools on the education of negroes, on their social attitudes and their prospects in the community at large. It could also be argued that sociological studies have helped immensely in a more humane urban redevelopment, on both sides of the Atlantic. In short, sociological understanding can be applied positively for the greater good of the individual and society.

But the same sociological understanding can be used for destructive ends. Knowledge of group dynamics and of structures of prejudice can be applied most effectively by those who wish to promote and exacerbate intra-group hatred. In the 1930s the Nazis succeeded in whipping up anti-semitic animosity by cleverly using the tool of sociology. Armed with statistics showing how Jews occupied positions of power in practically every area of life, they hinted darkly of take-over bids, and deliberately raised the worst atavistic fears. In totalitarian countries sociological data can be used to promote human solidarity, every bit as effectively as it can be in democracies. It is sobering to realise that the same processes which generate consensus can be used by a social worker in a summer camp and by a communist brain-washer in a prison camp in Korea or China.

Max Weber, one of the founding fathers of sociology, was emphatic in his claim that the discipline was 'value free'. This does not mean that the sociologist as a person is without values, for it is almost impossible for any human being to exist without values. To be sure, the sociologist as an individual, a parent, or a member of a religious group, will have many values, but within the discipline of his subject he recognises only one value—that of scientific integrity. As a human being he has to struggle against his own emotional inclinations, but as a sociologist he recognises them as a bias which ought to be eliminated. Peter Berger's analogy may help to clarify this point, which is by no means an unimportant one. The good spy is one who respects accurate information, from whatever source, free of bias. If as a Nazi, or a Communist, his reporting is coloured by his ideological affiliations, or by a desire to please his superiors, he is a bad spy, and the information he gives is useless for his own side. The good spy reports what is there and is no respecter of persons. It is up to others to act on the basis of this knowledge. There is a sense in which the sociologist is a spy, investigating a certain social terrain. As an individual, he may deplore the increase in prostitution in certain areas of our cities, or the rising incidence of wife-swopping in suburbia, but whatever his own moral attitude is, he will report the facts accurately, as he finds them. This is the only sense in which, with Max Weber, we can speak of sociology as being 'value free'.

The Scope of Sociology

It is sometimes argued that the function of sociology is to study religion *sub specie temporis* while that of theology is to view it *sub specie aeternitatis*. This is far too facile a distinction for the very reason that religion, whatever else it may be, exists historically, and is practised within a particular community. The theologian is ill-advised to adopt a lofty attitude to sociology by regarding it as an ancillary discipline, useful for market research on church attendance and the social environment in which the institution is located. We must on no account forget that Christianity is a historical religion and that the theologian, long before he began studying theology, was an individual living within a sociocultural situation.

It goes without saying that sociology as an empirical discipline can study the rise and fall of church membership within a given community. It can compare and criticise the various ecclesiastical structures of the Christian church— the episcopalian system peculiar to Anglicans and Roman Catholics, the oligarchic form which marks Presbyterianism, the more democratic shape of Congregationalism. It can examine reasons why certain people favour a 'high' form of worship, while others—the sects for instance—are as a rule 'low' churchmen. It can argue, as Bryan Wilson does that the contemporary ecumenical concern is no more than a struggle for ecclesiastical survival. It is a last-ditch attempt to save the universal Church from becoming a mere sect in a predominantly secular society. This kind of sociological investigation may be quite 'harmless' and can be easily implemented for pragmatic ecclesiastical purposes. The worst that churchmen can expect from an approach of this kind is the discovery that fewer people go to church now than at the turn of the century, or that the social prestige of the clergy is not so high as it used to be. All this may be very interesting, even enlightening, but does it mark the limit of sociological study?

There are theologians who try to get round the difficulty by drawing attention to two complementary aspects of the Church. On the one hand the Church is an invisible reality, built on the invisible bonds of faith shared by individual and community alike. This act of belief on which the Church rests cannot be measured, quantified or caught within the net of sociological investigation. On the other there is a visible Church, an organised structure, a hierarchical community, and as such it can be an object of scientific enquiry. This point of view is not necessarily false, but it is guilty of drawing too sharp a distinction between the invisible and the visible Church. The protagonists of such a position forget that John Calvin emphasised that the invisible Church and the visible Church were not two separate realities, but one Church.

The truth is that it is impossible to fix strict limits to sociological investigation. This applies even to the Lord's Supper. In instituting this rite, Jesus united the spirit of the old Jewish tradition and that of the new within the framework of the Passover. In examining how Jesus did this the investigator, however pious his intentions may be, is engaging in some sort of sociology. He knows that the Word of God, addressed to us in the Lord's Supper, comes to us in a concrete historical situation. It may seem impious to suggest that not even the Sacraments are exempt from sociological scrutiny, but as long as their shape is conditioned historically, it is legitimate to examine how this came to be.

It is equally true that the doctrinal formulations of the Church have been culturally conditioned and have been couched in a particular language which can be subject to empirical study. Historians are prepared to admit that the Chalcedonian formula was shaped by a number of complicated historical and political factors. The same is more or less true of the historic document we call the Westminster Confession. It is indeed possible to argue that a sociology of dogmas, a sociology of confessions, a sociology of liturgies are appropriate fields of study. There is no holy of holies, no inaccessible shrine, no sacred taboo to which sociology is forbidden an entrance.

Sociology as a Tool

In his *Sociology of Protestantism* Roger Mehl argues most cogently that in the exercise of its pastoral ministry the Church can use sociology as a helpful tool. Referring to Fathers Godin and Daniel's book *La France, Pays de Mission*, he points out that sociology is now universally accepted as a tool of mission. In this connection it is significant that the Roman Catholic Church hardly ever undertakes a major evangelical campaign without first making thorough sociological surveys on a number of levels. But this passion for sociological research in the area of mission did not begin with the Roman Catholic Church. It actually originated in the USA where a good many decades ago clergymen were the real pioneers of the sociology of religion.

Throughout Christendom, or what remains of it, the Church has lost effective contact with the industrial masses. Sociology may prove a useful tool in enabling her to understand the reasons for this alienation and suggesting ways of recovery. Locally, sociological research may help the minister to understand the composition of his parish, instead of relying on vague impressions compounded of idealism and unexamined illusions. This is illustrated in a survey undertaken within a metropolitan parish in Hamburg by Reinhard Koster. It showed that the majority of members were drawn from groups that were poorly integrated into society, marginal beings, women over forty, widows, unemployed spinsters, etc. This kind of investigation raises the disturbing question whether the Church is in danger of becoming an ersatz society, catering for those who have found no real place in the big society.

In his disturbing book *The Suburban Captivity of the Churches*, Gibson Winter brings sociological understanding to bear on mission. The major American denominations have built new Churches in residential areas, on the fringes of great metropolitan centres. In doing this they are obeying no theological insight, only reacting to a purely demographic and sociological trend. As he climbs the ladder of economic success, the middle-class American flees the city and shuns the country. He settles in suburbia which combines the advantages of both city and country. The Churches follow this mass middle-class exodus and find themselves witnessing in zones of homogenous social groupings. Those who cannot afford to move, the Puerto Ricans and the Negroes, stay behind and are ministered to by the sects and coloured Churches.

Gibson Winter supports Will Herberg's argument that the Churches in America have become substitutes for various ethnic groups, providing them with the means of social integration and personal identity. Paradoxically, although these Protestant denominations preach salvation by grace alone, their gospel is contradicted by the hollow activism of their many bustling organisations. These suburban Churches, the purveyors of leisure time activities, become the mirrors of the economic and social milieu in which they are situated. They offer the laity, not authentic ministries, but a way of escape from their public and professional roles, through a religion of inwardness and pietistic comfort.

In the light of a merciless sociological critique Winter goes on to suggest positive lines of action on the part of the suburban Churches. They should look towards the city from which they have made their escape, and should cultivate a measure of responsibility for the poverty-ridden areas. Instead of mobilising members in suburbia for their own ends, they should train them to become ambassadors for the Christian faith in the places where they work. Thus it would follow that preaching would be orientated not towards comfort and conformity, but towards the social and political responsibility of the Church. Only a modest beginning has been made, but already sociological analysis has led to attempts to establish new ecclesiastical structures in industrial urban areas. Two of the most notable are in East Harlem Protestant Church and the Detroit Industrial Mission.

In what sense can sociology help the Church to witness more effectively in a secular morally pluralistic society? In his *Secularisation and Moral Change* Alasdair MacIntyre argues that it was not the decline of institutional religion, but the process of secularisation, that produced moral change in British society. Or to put it another way, the apparent irrelevance of the contemporary Church is the effect not the cause of ethical pluralism. Though I suspect MacIntyre of grinding a Marxist axe here and there, I still think his thesis should be carefully examined. He is surely right in saying that the types of Bishop or Judge who pronounce ex-cathedra on war, sexual morality and juvenile delinquency, as if they were a mouthpiece of an established moral authority, are just survival relics, Robinson Crusoes, isolated on some desert island. As we live in a society united, if at all, by brutal utilitarian necessities, it is pernicious to foster such illusions.

The task of sociology is to be an agent of disenchantment —a benign Machiavelli, stripping us of sanctified prejudices, starry-eyed utopianisms and exaggerated notions of the Church's relevance in contemporary society. For example, we may examine a most intriguing contradiction from both a sociological and theological perspective—the state of the Churches in British and American societies. In Britain, organised religion seems to be in a state of decline, bordering on death. In the USA, where technology is further advanced than anywhere else, the Church appears to be in a healthy condition. How do we explain this contradiction? Peter Berger offers us what seems to me to be a very convincing answer. The Churches in America are blooming not because they are reflecting the essential nature of the Christian faith, but because they are mirroring the ambiguous values of a secular society. The paradox of religion in the USA, according to Berger, is that of social functionality with that of social irrelevance. It bestows its benedictions on certain values which belong to the secular fabric of American life.

One such value is success. This is not particularly American. It is deeply embedded in Western civilisation, and is highly cherished in Scotland. Our educational system is built on it and even within the Church we worship at its all-powerful shrine. Another central value is that of activism. The mystic, the contemplative, the man of prayer are at a disadvantage in our clock-dominated society. A vacancy committee on the prowl is not remotely interested in a scholarly saint; it prefers to chase after the monstrosity we euphemistically call 'a live wire'. Another prominent value is that of social adjustment. It finds expression in what Riesman calls the 'other directed character' and Whyte the 'Organisation Man'. The first Christians were known as disturbers of the peace but contemporary Christians are stigmatised as dedicated props of the *status quo*. The prophetic tradition so prominent in the Bible has been replaced by the politics of social accommodation. The rebel, the eccentric, the non-conformist is sadly out of place in the OK world of mass manipulation.

In inverse ratio to its functional success, organised religion is irrelevant to the major social issues which clamour for attention. This is one reason why men like Bishop Huddleston, Martin Luther King and Dietrich Bonhoeffer have made such an impression even on people who would not call themselves Christian. This admiration springs out of the awareness, however inarticulate, that religion possesses a prophetic dimension, and that there is such a thing as the sacred duty of maladjustment. The social witness of the Christian community is not a political but a theological imperative. Hendrik Kraemar affirms that the Church is mission. Perhaps the formulation is too one-sided. But what is true is that the meaning of the Church is endangered when the prophetic dimension is dissolved within the vacuum of social irrelevance.

The task of meaningful social engagement on the part of the Church may be as unrewarding as the efforts of Sisyphus in the myth. Nevertheless it is an imperative Christians must obey at all costs. In this kind of involvement there are no gimmicks, no organisational blueprint, no generally valid formulae. Those who undertake this work must have a theological grasp of the meaning of the Church, and equally important, theological understanding must be accompanied by empirical perception. It is not enough to have a doctrine of the Church. It is also necessary to have a sociology of the empirically existing churches. It is out of this inescapable tension between Christian doctrine on the one hand and sociological diagnosis on the other that an authentic Christian perspective is likely to emerge. The diagnosis without the doctrine may only lead to resignation, but the doctrine without empirical evidence may lead only to illusion—which is worse.

15. IMPERATIVES OF MISSION

The secular age has come. On all sides it proclaims its message confidently, boldly, even boisterously. The state has unshackled itself from the dominance of religion. Science has long since liberated itself from the concerns of faith. Art, which used to be the handmaiden of the Church, now regards her touch as the very touch of death. Industry, controlling so much of our lives, goes its merry way, producing, profiteering, advertising, paying not the slightest regard to religious scruples. Education, which in the past owed so much to the Church, glories in its autonomy. In short, the basic concerns of man's spirit carry no more than an attenuated relationship to religion. The world, in most areas, seems to operate very well without recourse to religious faith. It is no longer a consistent or a pervasive element of our life.

The world in which we are called upon to prosecute the mission of the Church is one which has been stripped of the supernatural, scrubbed clean of miracle, and deprived of a *Deus ex machina*—a problem-solving God—a very present aid in time of trouble. Ambiguity still shrouds Bonhoeffer's famous phrase 'man come of age', but whatever its meaning there is a sense in which adulthood has been thrust upon us whether we are ready for it or not. In a post-atomic space age we can no longer take refuge in sacred niches where we are visited by direct epiphanies. We are inhabitants of a secular world and if they are to be effective our strategies of mission must be geared into this kind of understanding.

The first Christians believed that the Church was the new humanity in Christ. 'As in Adam all die, so in Christ all are made alive', said Paul, affirming thereby that the whole of mankind is to be refashioned by the gracious purpose of the God who disclosed himself in the Event of Jesus. For the early Church, the crowning test of discipleship and indeed of membership into the new community was love. Within the new humanity in Christ all estranging barriers are broken down. 'There is neither Jew nor Greek, bond nor free, male or female, for ye are all one in Christ Jesus.' What an amazing picture of the Church is presented to us by the apostle Paul. As barriers of hatred, conflict and mistrust characterised the old humanity, so *koinonia*—forbearance in love and unity in the Spirit—is the animating life of the new community.

It is this vision of the new humanity more than any other which creates the dynamic for the mission of the Church. In this understanding, Christ has come not to save an elite few but all the children of men—irrespective of class, nation or race. Therefore the Church is called upon to proclaim a universal gospel and to open its doors wide to every living human creature. Since the people of God are in principle the whole of humanity the task of mission can never cease. Any church that has lost the impulse of seeking the lost beyond its boundaries, as well as the lost within them, has to that extent ceased to be faithful to the commission entrusted to it.

Mission is a necessary and indeed an all-important activity of the Church; nevertheless I am inclined to agree with Professor Langdon Gilkey that mission does not constitute the Church's inner essence. There are two reasons for this. For one thing, if people concentrate solely or even mainly on making other people Christians, they are apt to cease being concerned about their own relationship with God. For another thing, if the Church is primarily concerned with expanding its membership there is apt to be nothing substantial there when the new convert is finally persuaded to join. The Dutch Reformed Church in South Africa and the Southern Baptists in the USA enthusiastically sponsor missionary programmes, but are not noted for their crusading zeal against apartheid. Important as is the passing on of the faith to others, nevertheless that faith itself must consist of more than the process of passing it on. A relay team whose members themselves never ran but only handed on the baton to other runners would win no races. Similarly a Church whose main ambition is to add to its roll ceases to be the Church.

Concern for humanity is the dynamic behind mission but next in importance is the need to understand our world and to become engaged with it in a meaningful way. Christians may resent a pluralistic secular culture, but it is precisely in such a context that they are called to witness to the Lordship of Jesus Christ. Dedication is imperative, but it is not enough. Commitment must go hand in hand with hard-headed analysis and clear perception. In order to grasp the Herculean task that modern mission is called to undertake we have first of all to assess the importance of the seismic upheavals that have shaken our society over the last two centuries or so. In passing let me refer to some of them.

(1) *The Exodus of the Workers*

Perhaps the most important single event in the history of modern Christianity was the departure of the working masses from the church. Various reasons have been advanced to explain their exodus, each one of which no doubt contains a large modicum of the truth. The parish structure, it is said, was first adapted to a rural population and in a rapidly expanding urban society it became more and more irrelevant. This is illustrated by what happened in the city of Birmingham. In 1801 the population was approximately 74,000. By 1821 it had risen to 107,000, yet only one new church had been erected in the city since 1779. This shows not only a serious defect in the parish system as first envisaged, but also ineptness on the part of the institutional Church itself. The truth is that even if the disgruntled working masses wanted to worship, there was no place for them to do so.

But perhaps a profounder reason for the mass exodus was

the identification of the church with the ruling élites of European society. In the past these élites were the mortal enemies of the workers and the workers knew it. Since then, to be sure, startling advances have been made, but the memory of bygone days has ploughed deep and our strident and self-conscious humanitarian efforts are powerless to efface it. The working masses refuse religious communion with those that denied them brotherhood.

This exodus must weigh heavily upon the Christian conscience. This is so, not merely because God himself became incarnate in a working man, the Carpenter of Nazareth, but because organised Christianity in the West has become predominantly a middle-class phenomenon. The truncated remnant of the faithful is dominated by one class. This is tragic not merely because it is a denial of the meaning of the Incarnation, but because the Church, riddled with middle-class fastidiousness, has lost the emotional spontaneity and the exuberant vitality so characteristic of the working man. In an age when he is gaining power and influence by means of collective bargaining, it is imperative to have him inside the church.

(2) *The Alienation of the Intellectuals*
This, too, has been a gradual process and is a consequence of the ascendancy—one is almost tempted to say the omnipotency—of modern science. The scientific temper is all-pervasive and has seeped into every corner and cranny of our thinking. Unknown to us, it conditions our values, moulds our day-to-day behaviour, and shapes our attitude to the entire universe. The implications of the scientific revolution are not sufficiently stressed in Christian thought, and the so-called New Intellectual proclaiming his atheistic philosophy through the media of the novel, drama and television constitutes a menace, the seriousness of which has not yet been fully grasped.

The New Intellectual proceeds on the assumption that God is a displaced person. He has been displaced not only from the universe but from the individual consciousness as well, and he is no longer necessary as a working hypothesis. The gaps in man's experience which in former days required the intervention of *Deus ex machina* have now been bridged and explained. Diseases that once decimated entire populations have been mastered, extreme poverty has been eliminated and the sharpness of the sting of death has been softened by the rise in pain-killing drugs. The prestige of science is enormous because it succeeds, it works, it does things. The modern man believes that, given time, it will solve every problem.

The New Intellectual, on the whole, is impervious to the traditional methods of evangelism. The God we offer him must be big enough to cope not merely with the isolated problems of the individual experience, but with the total problem of existence. A God wrapped up in a medieval or pre-Copernican theology is anathema to him. He does not claim omniscience, but he does ask serious and searching questions and, if we are to convince him that Christ is the Truth, we must try to answer him as intelligently and as sincerely as we know how.

(3) *The Crisis Among the Young*

Marcuse maintains that the young intellectuals are the spearhead and vanguard of the revolutionary movements of the present time. This is not strictly true. In the Black Power Movement in the USA and the Civil Rights Movement in North Ireland there are many involved who are not students in any formal sense of that word. While this is so, the majority of marchers are young adults in their teens, twenties and early thirties. It is perhaps salutary to remember that the young—that is to say, those under twenty-five years of age— constitute more than fifty per cent of the world's population.

The young are convinced that the most liberal of institutions and the most enlightened of men in modern society, when confronted by the demand for change, resort to forceful means of compelling consent. The crisis is not a decision to retrace the footsteps of mankind. It is rather a decision to remake what man has already made—society. The young are gripped by the vision that man can create his own future. This is the essential optimism of the twentieth century. The young share it and they are determined to use it.

The *cri de coeur* is for justice at all levels in social, economic and political relationships. The young today stand, in the lineage of faith, with the children of Israel in Egypt and like their ancestors in Israel are preparing themselves for the long march out of Egypt into the promised land. When that long march happens, the powers that be, like the Pharoahs, will not be able to say 'You did not tell us'. They have been telling us in the shape of teach-ins, sit-downs and highly publicised marches. The protests of today correspond to the plagues of Egypt.

The crisis relates to the vision of a new life in the promised land. It is concerned with better housing, greater beauty in our towns, better education enabling man to do justice to all his innate possibilities, the remaking of our cultural and spiritual life, so that these accord with the hopes and expectations of mankind. The charter for the new world has not yet appeared. The old models—liberal, capitalist, democratic, communistic—are rejected. The new models— Mao's China and Castro's Cuba—are viewed tentatively and critically. This confrontation between the young and the old, constitutes the matrix out of which the new world will emerge.

In terms of Evangelism, what does the crisis among the young look like through the lens of Christian experience. Perhaps we should not be unduly surprised that there are certain expressions of the crisis which correspond to an uncanny degree to the perennial crisis of the Christian faith itself. There is a universal vision, transcending all natural boundaries. There is a prophetic concern for justice. There is a willingness as with Abraham to leave comfortable securities behind, to break loose from our little Christendoms and to explore territories for which as yet we have no maps.

However misguided, these are genuine attempts to experience the life more abundant. And finally there is a growing sense of responsibility on the part of man for his dominion over the natural world and the proper use of its natural resources. It may be that I am over-optimistic but I see a great potential in the crisis among the young.

Enough of diagnosis. Let us now turn to the question of whether traditional techniques of Evangelism are relevant to the present situation. There is a crisis of mission, using the word 'crisis' in its Greek sense of decision, carrying with it overtones of choice and judgment. If Evangelism is the calling of men and women to a knowledge of Christ as Saviour and Lord, we must go on to ask if Christian conversion is dependent on our understanding of what God is doing in history. A preliminary task is to clarify our minds as to the difference between traditional revivalism and contemporary mission.

American revivalism has always been an exportable commodity, at least within the Anglo-Saxon world. On the whole its emphasis has been pietistic and its influence disappointingly evanescent. Professor William G. McLoughlin Jr., the American Church historian, claims that revivalism from Finney to Graham has contributed to the secularisation of American Protestantism. In order to woo the masses and to engineer mass consent, Revivalists had to resort to questionable gimmicks and a whole variety of dubious techniques. Ironically enough this resulted in the distortion of the very pietism they sponsored and the secularising of a faith which is supposed to be essentially spiritual.

The social emphasis of Anglo-Saxon revivalism has not been too obtrusive on the whole. To begin with Finney opposed the abolition of slavery and only came round when public opinion left him no option. Moody, himself of working class origin, moved into the middle classes and adapted his message to their *mores*. Billy Graham at first took up a neutral attitude to the problem of race and only relented when the Supreme Court denounced segregation as a sin.

British Revivalists have not been as colourful as their American counterparts but they have been equally pietistic. Their whole attitude to society has been based on a number of naïve assumptions and a set of theological presuppositions which many of us would regard as untenable. While harping on the essential depravity of human nature they reduced sin to simple individualistic proportions. The most complex and the most perverse of all problems, man's relationship to man in society, they simply ignored.

Revivalist theology disparages collective efforts at reform. Since all sin is individualistic, reform by that very token must be individualistic too. Regeneration, not legislation, changes the human heart and until that is changed all else is useless. Traditional Revivalism loudly condemned liberal optimism but was itself guilty of shallow utopianism, because it assumed that its own particular brand of Evangelism was the cure for all problems. In ignoring the complexity of social sin and in remaining blind to the devious subtlety of individual motivation, Revivalism was also guilty of escapism. It has this in common with the M.R.A. Movement—a grotesque over-simplification of the maddening ambiguities of human existence, coupled with grandiose claims which fail to stand up to serious scrutiny.

The Church must be prepared to dissociate herself from discredited patterns of Evangelism which are about as useful as the long bow in the post-atomic age. Where mission is concerned there is genuine ambiguity which sometimes joins forces with downright dishonesty. A prominent New York minister once confessed to me that while he was deeply suspicious of Billy Graham's approach, he was forced into a position where he had to give him public support. A Church that indulges in this kind of double think will pay dearly for it. The kind of Evangelism that is pietistic and world-despising, coupled with a bang up-to-date publicity, can only succeed in projecting a disastrous image of the Christian faith. It is not possible to communicate the Gospel till people begin to ask the questions to which Christianity is the answer.

The Church must participate with the industrial masses in their sense of insecurity before they can begin to speak meaningfully to them. Similarly Christians and agnostics must wrestle with the same agonising problems before they can understand one another. Amid the darkness of mission we have at least one glimmer of light—without participation there can be no communication.

BIOGRAPHICAL AND BIBLIOGRAPHICAL NOTES TO PART FIVE: THE MINISTER AS PROPHET

13. INVOLVEMENT IN POLITICS

William Golding
The modern novelist who takes human sin seriously. Man's capacity for destructive violence and his devouring pride are vividly depicted in *The Lord of the Flies* and in *The Spire*.

Roland Bainton
Professor of Ecclesiastical History in Yale University, USA. A dedicated pacifist, he argues eloquently against the possession and proliferation of nuclear weapons. His best-known work is perhaps his biography of Luther, *Here I Stand*.

John C. Bennett
Emeritus President of Union Theological Seminary, New York. Following Reinold Niebuhr he is perhaps the most outstanding Christian exponent of applying theological insights to our social and political ambiguities. This is illustrated by two of his books, *Christians and the State* and *Christian Social Action*.

14. PLACE OF SOCIOLOGY

Max Weber
The distinguished German sociologist who has exercised such a far-reaching influence on modern sociological investigation. His

most famous and most widely quoted work is *The Protestant Ethic and the Spirit of Capitalism*.

Peter Berger
An American sociologist who tries to relate the insights of theology to sociology. His best-known works are *The Social Reality of Religion* and *The Noise of Solemn Assemblies*.

Gibson Winter
Professor of Ethics and Society in Chicago University, he has shown a special concern for the task of Christian mission in a secularised, urbanised society. His best-known works are *The New Creation as Metropolis* and *The Suburban Captivity of the Churches*.

Bryan Wilson
An Oxford sociologist who has studied the sociological side of religion in both America and England (not Scotland). Pessimistic about the future of the Institutional Church, he is also sceptical about the rise of ecumenicism. His best-known work is *Religion in Secular Society*.

15. IMPERATIVES OF MISSION

Herbert Marcuse
A German social philosopher who emigrated to Switzerland and later to America. His analysis of the predicament of man in modern society has been a source of revolutionary ideas and slogans. His best-known work is *One Dimensional Man*.

William G. McLoughlin Jr.
Professor of History and American Civilization at Brown University. He is one of the leading authorities on American revival tradition. His best-known works are *Modern Revivalism* and *Billy Graham (Revivalist in a Secular Age)*.

Conclusion

SHAPE OF THINGS TO COME

SHAPE OF THINGS TO COME

In the Old Testament there is a tragic story of a man of God, sent to prophesy to Jeroboam at Bethel. This he does with commendable courage, till an older man, almost certainly an establishment figure, decides to intervene. The prophet lost his nerve, betrayed the word he had hitherto so faithfully proclaimed and, running foul of the power structures of the day, was mercilessly liquidated. The story may have grown in the telling but no matter how much it may have been embellished it warns us that prophecy is a dangerous business. God's word cannot fail in its ultimate purpose, but the man who toys with it, or betrays it, does so at his own peril.

The true prophet is not someone brimming over with self confidence, glorying in his assumed role, secure in the knowledge that he shares the councils of God. On the contrary, more than most men he is aware of the uncertainties and the vast imponderables which belong to the very stuff of history. Misreading the situation may lead to tragedy as it did for the prophet who incurred the displeasure of Jeroboam. Hence the reluctance of men like Amos and Jeremiah to assume the prophetic office. To expect people to come to terms with reality or to read the future with creative sensitivity is to ask a great deal. The great prophets were aware of this to the point of agony. It is not surprising then, that even to this day, it is generally accepted that the mark of the authentic prophet is the courage to say hard things.

History teaches us many lessons and one of them is the stubborn resistance to change shared by individuals and groups alike. The politician who sets out to debunk wicked ideologies, the educationist who wishes to introduce new

171

teaching methods, the minister of religion who experiments with new forms of worship, find themselves in violent collision with the built-in conservatism endemic in persons and institutions. Earnest intellectuals who bravely talk of 'educating for change' and preparing the masses for the future, little realise how difficult it is for the majority of men and women to adapt themselves to the strange and the unknown.

The tough, hard-headed realist who boasts of living in the present is sadly out of date. The apostles of 'presentism' are a dying breed. They are the two-legged dinosaurs of our time, about to perish from the face of the earth. In Europe and America, go-ahead corporations pay large salaries to intuitive futurists. They are not asking for accurate scientific forecasts but for mind-stretching speculations about future possibilities. And more than the big industrial combines, the Church needs a multiplicity of visions, a succession of dreams and prophecies, a profusion of images of potential tomorrows. What Christianity needs today is not a host of bogus futurologists, but an army of men and women who march purposefully with the future in their bones. In the words of H. G. Wells, they are so sensitive to the present, that already they can anticipate 'the shape of things to come'.

(1) *The Shape of the Church*

From the very beginning of the Church there have been divisions, and at the same time movements to demonstrate the oneness of the Body of Christ. From the time of Paul it could be said that a minority of Christians have not been happy about the disunity of a Church that professed Jesus Christ as Lord. In the twentieth century and particularly in the second half, this conscience has become more sharp and imperious. More and more, Christians are coming to see that a situation where denominations confessing the same Lord are not in communion, deserves no other name than blasphemy or sin.

In his *Religion in a Secular Society* Bryan Wilson, the Oxford sociologist, sets out to debunk the ecumenical movement. He argues that organisations amalgamate when they are weak, not when they are strong. The clergy are keener on ecumenicism than the laity and that for various reasons. As their social status in a secular society progressively declines, they instinctively form an alliance which leaps across denominational lines. Robbed of their traditional roles as educationist, counsellor, welfare officer, they have strategically retreated to a citadel from which the forces of secularism cannot dislodge them. In this ivory tower the clergy can enhance their own status, cultivate their own universe of discourse and display their own esoteric specialised competence.

The answer to Bryan Wilson's attack is the historical witness of the Church. Clement of Alexandria claimed that the true Church is one. Cyprian is even more outspoken in his condemnation of disunity. Every major father and doctor of the Church, throughout its chequered history— Augustine, Luther, Calvin, Zwingli, Erasmus, Knox, Wesley—has known that the Church is one because the Lord is one. Karl Barth, the most illustrious theologian of this century, is under no sectarian illusion when he writes 'The plurality of the churches, of which we find no trace in the New Testament, is in the light of the nature of the church, of the Body of Christ, ontologically if you like, impossible. It is only possible as sin is possible'.

But can we discern any recognisable shape to the emerging Church? For those who have eyes to see there are certain signs of hope. In 1929 the majority of Presbyterians in Scotland came together in a united Church of Scotland. In 1935 in Canada, Presbyterians, Methodists and Congregationalists joined, to form the United Church of Canada. In 1947 these same three traditions, along with the Anglicans, formed the United Church of South India. In 1972 Presbyterians and Congregationalists in England joined forces to form the United Reformed Church. Those unions may seem trivial in comparison with the size of the challenge confronting the institutional Church. But on the other hand they would have been inconceivable apart from a spirit of self-criticism within the institution and the thrust of a new radicalism among Christians of different traditions.

It would be foolish to dogmatise, or to attempt to describe in any precise way the form of the future Church. History is a dynamic process which has a habit of confounding our most confident predictions. While many questions remain unanswered, and will be so till the end of time, on the basis of sociological research it seems better not to merge all worshippers into one monolithic structure. A variety of religious communities can appeal to different temperaments and different classes. Bryan Wilson is correct in drawing our attention to the secular pressures pounding away at the Church. What he fails to see is that God, in the same way as he used Cyrus the dictator in the Old Testament, can use secularism to promote the oneness of the Church he instituted in Christ.

The Christian faith, no matter what Malcolm Muggeridge and his fellow Docetists say, cannot exist as a disembodied belief or as a distilled ethic. It must take unto itself a body in the shape of definite structures. At the same time we must be prepared to be outrageously agnostic about particular structures. In his *Church Order in the New Testament* Eduard Schweizer claims that the early Church's effectiveness was related to its flexible ecclesiastical systems. The structures were always subservient to mission. In Asia Minor and elsewhere, as the Church expanded, the structures were intelligently adapted to particular cultural situations. Once Christians abandon their idolatries and stop absolutising that which is merely relative, authentic unity is under way. We can confidently predict that before the turn of this century, Papacy, Episcopacy and Presbyterianism will be subjected to the most ruthless scrutiny. Provided the Church takes mission seriously there is no reason why a number of ecclesiastical structures should not co-exist in a pluralistic society.

(2) *The Shape of the Congregation*

In the report on 'Priorities of Mission in the 70s' submitted
to the General Assembly of the Church of Scotland in 1971,
the most controversial suggestion was perhaps the one which
advocated larger groupings than that of the congregation.
Communicants are asked to regard themselves not as
members of a local church, standing at some street corner,
but as members of the Church in Glasgow, in Edinburgh,
in Aberdeen or Dundee. No doubt the Commission responsible for this report was reacting against a petty-minded
parochialism which elevates the congregation into a position
of supreme importance. Whatever sympathy we can muster
for this kind of innovation we are bound to ask whether such
a strategy amounts to no more than ecclesiological utopianism.

There is one stubborn fact which the architects of change
disregard at their own peril. For most Christians the form of
the Church which means anything to them is the congregation. What is more, we can safely wager that any departure
from such a structure will be vehemently resisted. This is
implied in the most radical literature on the subject calling
for a revitalisation of the congregation. It is indeed the
theme of several studies that have become classics! *The Face
of my Parish* (Tom Allan), *Revolution in a City Parish* (Abbé
Michouneau), *The Parish comes Alive* (Ernest Southcott). In
his book *The New Shape of American Religion*, Martin Marty
writes, 'We already possess the institutions we need to
undertake the religious task, set before America today'.

But do we? This is a crucial question for modern mission.
The parent denomination and all the members thereof
expect the congregation to have its own building. This means
that from the start the minister is involved in a double
activity—that of increasing the membership, and of raising
as much money as possible. Statistically, the growth of a
congregation can be plotted in terms of two indices: a
demographic and a fiscal one. Once this kind of ecclesiastical
enterprise is embarked on, there are relentless pressures

ranging from the crude to the subtle to justify it. The moment it is established the apparatus clamours for attention and maintenance takes precedence over mission.

Let me put it as succinctly as I can. The sharp edge of Christian engagement with the world is unlikely to be the local congregation. This does not mean that we can write off the congregation as a useless anachronism. Heaven forbid! In the task of preaching and teaching, of nurturing the faithful by means of word and sacrament, it is irreplaceable. But in the task of meaningful engagement with a secular world, the potentialities of the local congregation can only be viewed with pessimism. What we need for such a task are supra-parochial patterns or settings. The trend seems to be in the direction of the larger group or better still the 'ecumenical parish'. Bluntly it means that the local congregation has to abandon any illusion it may have to make an impact on the larger community. It further means that the various strategies of social engagement with the world—Christian service, Christian action, Christian dialogue—are the concern of the wider supra-parochial setting.

What about smaller groups within the congregation itself? Needless to say we must guard against artificial groups whose sole purpose in coming together is the realisation that the congregation is too big and impersonal. We need some theological justification for the creation of such groups and we do not have far to look. In his letter to the Corinthians Paul writes 'Acquilla and Priscilla, together with the Church in their house, send you hearty greetings in the Lord'. There is considerable evidence that within the first few centuries Christianity was simply honeycombed with small groups which never regarded themselves as separate, but as belonging to the whole Church. This cellular structure has a long history behind it. It can only be revitalised and made to work if it adapts itself flexibly and spontaneously to the social realities of a particular community. Thus the various structures—the congregation, the cell in industry, in education, in the arts, the house Church and the supra-parochial setting—far from witnessing as rivals could mutually reinforce one another. They are capable of making a terrific impact on the world.

(3) *The Shape of the Ministry*

The parish ministry is not the only pattern we have inherited from the past. There were others. In the medieval Church there were priests who were engaged in teaching and administrative work, corresponding roughly to what is done by specialist ministries today. The Reformers emphasised the primacy of the pastoral ministry, but they made exceptions of theological teachers and military chaplains. In the Independent Churches there was a greater emphasis on the itinerant than on the settled ministry. This proved particularly successful in fluid situations, such as the settlement of the American frontier. This is beyond dispute, but there are still ministers and laymen who regard the parish pattern as the only valid ministry. Other ministries in education and industry they are prepared to recognise but only in a subordinate capacity.

A Church that takes mission in a secular society seriously can no longer afford to oppose specialisation. The acceptance of this fact points in the direction of team ministries which in the future may come to be regarded as a norm rather than as an exception. Such team ministries should include a diversity of skills. Teachers, youth leaders, psychotherapists and social workers could pool their various expertise. And of course in such a team there ought to be a place for an ordained minister. The time has come to question the assumption that all a parish requires is one man trained in the traditional theological disciplines. To operate at his maximum efficiency, the ordained minister must be prepared to work with secular experts who bring their peculiar skills to the service of the Church.

If the isolation of the Church from the secular world is a major challenge, the acceptance of part-time ministers could be a step in the right direction. This would be much more than an ecclesiastical device for taking services of worship during a shortage of professionals. It could be a strategy aimed at serving both Church and world by the recognition of men who carry about with them tensions, stemming from allegiance to both. There is nothing either in the New Testament or in the Reformed conception of the ministry that precludes such a possibility. This part-time pattern would have the effect of strengthening, not diluting, the ministry of the Church. One of our problems is not the dearth but the calibre of candidates offering themselves for the ministry. If we could only communicate the fact that the ministry must not be identified with an élitist set called the clergy, but with the whole body of believers, then our hand would be immeasurably strengthened. We need good men, drawn from every walk of life, in order to project a robust image of the ministry in what remains of this century.

The role of part-time ministries would not do away with the need for specialised professionals, though not primarily in local churches. In a complex society, more science-dominated and more industry-shapen than ever before, there is a greater call for a diversified ministry. If the Church is to witness with any degree of relevance in the world of culture there must be a profusion of experiments in new forms of ministry. These experiments must consider tactics which will reach those who mould our tastes, shape our thinking and take the decisions that affect the future of our society. Ministries of this kind demand a thorough theological training combined with awareness of economic and social problems.

It goes without saying that new forms of ministry do not make superfluous the role of the professional clergy serving a local church. The suburb must be ministered to as well as the slum. The work involved in teaching, befriending and caring pastorally for thousands of people, whether in suburbia or down-town, does justify the full-time occupation of a theologically educated man set aside for the purpose. In a society becoming increasingly secular in its attitudes and more and more educated, the total communication of our knowledge of God, must not be left exclusively in the hands of amateurs.

The question of ordination is being posed by an increasing number of theological students, laymen and young ministers all over the world. Some of them feel that of all the Church's doctrines, this one stands most in need of demythologising. They argue that in terms of the Church's ministry and mission to the world, the concept of ordination is no longer helpful or meaningful. The status conferred on a minister on ordination and the mystique that surrounds it is all wrong, they say. Writers like Hans Ruedi Weber (*The Militant Ministry*) and Professor Hanson (*The Pioneer Ministry*) have faced up to this knotty problem. While the positions they advocate are interesting and provocative I feel certain that ordination and the many problems connected with it calls for more historical research and theological probing. Broadly speaking, there are two views of the ministry. One is that the whole body of believers possess the primary ministry while the minority of the ordained clergy is secondary. Professor John MacQuarrie favours the view that the ordained ministry is primary and must not be assimilated into the general ministry. The truth is that at the moment the 'quest for the historical ministry' seems as hopeless as the quest for the historical Jesus. Any attempt to establish a definite ministerial structure is not likely to meet with much success. Whatever the truth about ordination, the ministry of the Church engaged in mission must have a measure of flexibility and healthy untidiness to allow for development and adaptation within an overall pattern.

(4) *Shape of Theological Education*
The content of the Christian message (which is the subject matter of preaching) and the sense of the presence of God (which is the concern of worship) are not at all easy to communicate in a secularised age. But if the truth about God is of paramount importance we must be prepared to go to

any length to convey it to a desperately needy world. If someone were suddenly to discover the cure for cancer he could not keep the news to himself but would shout the stupendous news from the house tops. Plants would go up in record time to produce the miracle stuff which, for the whole of humanity, would literally mean the difference between life and death. And if the Christian Gospel is the answer to the human malaise, its advocates must be in the grip of a similar compulsion.

Jean Paul Sartre felt he had a liberating message for the whole of humanity. God was dead, so man had to arrogate to himself the powers and attributes which formerly belonged to the Deity. As his own saviour man has to create values which would enable him to live in freedom in the midst of ultimate meaninglessness. A philosopher, Sartre knew he could only reach a limited coterie as a university teacher, so he set out to master two strange media of communication— that of the drama and of the novel. Through them, he has been able to reach millions of his contemporaries. If an atheist is prepared to take communication with such passionate seriousness how much more the Christian theologian who believes he has a message of supreme importance for the whole of mankind.

This does not mean that theology has to surrender the technical vocabulary, which any discipline aspiring to scientific status must necessarily possess. In the pursuit of truth the theologian must inevitably cultivate a stance of detachment. Like a doctor making a blood test or an x-ray examination he has for the time being to abandon his commitment to people whose fate is in his hands. On such a level, detachment is not only legitimate but highly desirable. It is precisely because this kind of objectivity is so important that the theologian must avoid getting mired down in methodology or getting lost in the jungle of hermeneutics. It is possible to be coldly analytical and at the same time to be passionately involved in the human predicament. Bertrand Russell is the example *par excellence*.

Total involvement demands a high degree of cognitive awareness and a large measure of moral courage. So many of us are palaeolithic in art, neanderthal in politics, victorian in morals, and only modern in our plumbing and accountancy. We need men who understand secular culture and can communicate it articulately to others. Theologians must be as sensitive as the dramatist, the poet or the novelist. They dare not be less rigorous than the scientist and they must be at least as concerned with people as the psychiatrist. Courageously they must enter into the structures of anxiety, guilt and alienation which in varying degrees they too share with all men. Where there is no participation there is no communication.

Theology cannot cut itself adrift from the concerns of the individual. Man's limits, weaknesses and boundary concerns have not yet been conquered. Existential anxiety is ever with us and we are all looking for some ultimate horizon of meaning which will make sense of life. Death is still the last enemy and guilt is our constant companion. These are facts that cannot be ignored, but attention should also be given to Bonhoeffer's warning. He accuses theology of an unhealthy preoccupation with man's inwardness, and a dangerous disregard of his outwardness. To put it another way, he accuses theology of being more concerned with man's confining limits than with his beckoning possibilities. Man possesses powers to land him on the moon, to change the face of nature, and to transform (physically at least) the whole of society. This means that if theology takes the doctrine of man seriously, it cannot opt out of the sphere of collective responsibility. On no account must we underestimate the power of economics to change patterns of human behaviour and to eject tenaciously-held prejudices from the minds of individuals and communities. It is very probable that at the end of the day apartheid will be overcome not by the perspectives of Christian theology but by the pressures of economics.

In the past the structures of the Church were geared to

cope with a theology of inwardness, with questions of guilt, meaninglessness and death. In the present the Church is ill-equipped to deal with the direction in which a theology of outwardness is moving—Christian responsibility in the midst of technological, political and social change. In face of this kind of revolution, the fanatical defence of established patterns of Church life amount to a flight from responsibility. As Christians we are called upon to discover new structures and new strategies which will help us to communicate the Gospel in the public sector as well as in the private. If it is to remain in business, Christian theology must concern itself with the responsible use of power.

BIOGRAPHICAL AND BIBLIOGRAPHICAL NOTES TO CONCLUSION: SHAPE OF THINGS TO COME

Eduard Schweizer

Professor of New Testament in the University of Zurich. Since he was brought up as a Baptist it is interesting to note the large area of agreement between him and Professor Hans Küng, the radical Roman Catholic theologian. This is particularly so on the question of the nature of the ministry. His best-known book is *Church Order in the New Testament*.

Docetists

They were the first known Christian heretics, appearing within the first century. They taught that Christ had no real physical body, no real human nature, but only an apparent body. They were rejected because such a belief denies the meaning of the Incarnation.

Jean Paul Sartre

The distinguished French existentialist philosopher, novelist and dramatist. Like Camus he sponsors a philosophy of the absurd. His best-known books are *The Age of Reason, Iron in the Soul, Nausea* and *No Exit*.